Critical Thinking
for College Students
Third edition

Denise Albert

Printed in Canada

ISBN 978-0-9738997-2-6

For more information or to order book contact: info@accescible-editions.com

Acknowledgments

I would like to thank Virginie Bilodeau for her moral support and patience in the creation of this third edition as well as Robert Lemay, who gracefully agreed to review all the exercises that were added.

As with the previous two editions, many thanks to Champlain College students for inspiring and motivating me to provide them with non-expensive educational material. And since a third edition cannot exist without its predecessors, continuous credit should be given to Alison Tett, Jean Lachapelle, Bruce Toombs, Jim Morris, Marie-Josée Katcho, Kory Goldberg and Sophie Doré, for their valuable help in the creation and editing of the previous editions of this book.

TABLE OF CONTENT

1. WHY STUDY CRITICAL THINKING?
What is critical thinking? 6
When will this skill be useful? 7

2. ARGUMENT
Definition 9
Premise 9
Conclusion 9
Standardized form 10
STRUCTURE OF AN ARGUMENT
How to recognize an argument 10
Premise indicators 13
Conclusion indicators 13
NOT AN ARGUMENT
Series of facts 14
Emotions 14
Series of questions 15
Descriptions 16
Explanations 16
ACTIVITY 1 **18**
CHAPTER EXERCISES **20**

3. DEDUCTIVE LOGIC
Validity 23
Soundness 30
ACTIVITY 2 **33**
CHAPTER EXERCISES **35**

4. INDUCTIVE ARGUMENTS
Difference between inductive and deductive logic 38
Deductive or inductive logic? 40
ACTIVITY 3 **42**
CHAPTER EXERCISES **43**

5. TRUTH OF A PREMISE
Supported by a good sub-argument 45
A priori true 46
Common knowledge 46
Supported by a relevant figure of authority 47
ACTIVITY 4 **48**
UNACCEPTABLE PREMISE
Counter example 49
A priori false 49
Contradicting premises 49
Ambiguity 50
Premise needs justification/ Faith and intuitions 50
ACTIVITY 5 **51**
CHAPTER EXERCISES **52**

6. FALLACIES
False dilemma 54
Ignorance 55
Equivocation 55
Begging the question – Circularity 56
Appeal to pity 56
Popularity 57
Ad hominem 58
Hasty generalization 58
Red Herring 59
Slippery slope 59
ACTIVITY 6 **61**
CHAPTER EXERCISES **63**

7. UNDERSTANDING STATISTICS
Unreliable statistic 65
Confusing average 67
Proving one thing, concluding another 68
Deceiving by omitting information 69
Year of sample 70
Size of sample 70
Biased sample 70
Research methods 71
ACTIVITY 7 **73**
CHAPTER EXERCISES **74**

8. ANALYZING A THESIS ESSAY 78
Read essay 78
Find conclusion of the argument 78
Find the premises 79
Write the argument in standardized form 79
Determine whether the argument is valid 79
Identify assumptions 79
Establish truth of each premise 81
Differentiate between fact and opinion 81
Determine the quality of the argument 82
Give your overall comments on the argument 82
ACTIVITY 8 (Truth about ASR tires essay) **83**
CHAPTER EXERCISES (essays) **86**
-*The contemporary relevance of Greek mythology* 86
-*Pablo Picasso's value* 88
-*The hijab: confusing religion and culture* 90
-*The truth about cell phones* 92
-*Vaccination is the disease, not the cure* 94

9. HOW TO WRITE A THESIS ESSAY
Finding a topic 96
Doing research 97
Creating a thesis statement 99
Writing an essay outline 101
Writing an introduction 103
Writing a paragraph 105
Writing a conclusion 108
Visualizing an essay 108
Essay checklist 111

APPENDIX: Answers to selected exercises 114

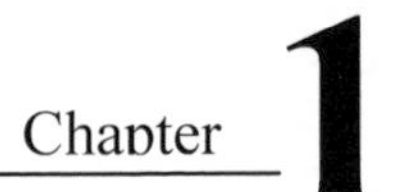

WHY STUDY CRITICAL THINKING?

What is critical thinking?

Being a strong critical thinker means that you question information, that you can assess the relationship between different ideas and that you can create new coherent links between them. One of the main components of critical thinking is to be able to evaluate and create arguments in hopes that you will not buy every idea that is sold to you. Being a critical thinker does not mean that you have opinions. It means that you can **defend** your opinions using the various rules of reasoning.

Although some associate the word 'critical' with 'fault finding', in this context, critical thinking refers to the ability to analyze and evaluate. For example, there are art, film, music and sports' critics that express their opinions on the basis of standards.

Critical thinking is a skill. It is not a series of definitions that you can learn by heart. This book gives you the tools needed to be a good critical thinker and explains how to use each tool. However, just as with any skill, the only way to become good is to practice. For example, I can give you a hammer and a nail and explain how to hold the hammer and the nail and how to hammer your nail in. However, until you actually try and practice for yourself, you will not have the skill. The purpose of critical thinking and of this book is not for you to simply know about reasoning; it is to ensure that you actually apply this knowledge and that you BE a good critical thinker.

When will this skill be useful?

As a high school student, you were taught the building blocks of learning: how to read, how to count, a series of facts about history, geography, chemistry, physics and many other topics. However, there is much more to learning than being able to recite various facts. Ultimately, these facts can only be useful if we learn to interpret and synthesize them in order to create our own basis of knowledge.

When you read something in the newspaper or hear it on TV, do you question whether the information presented is true? Do you question if it is relevant? Do you question the source? Can you do more than regurgitate someone else's opinion? Can you actually formulate your own and justify it properly?

Here are a series of various concrete examples of when critical thinking skills would come in handy:

- It is Friday night and you want to borrow the car from your parents. If you are lucky, they will give you a simple 'yes' upon your asking. But if your parents are anything like mine were, you will have to **convince** them to lend you the car.

- Your partner or you, unexpectedly become pregnant and you must decide what you want to do. Should you keep the baby? Give it up for adoption? Get an abortion? You will need to explain and **justify** your decision to your partner and most importantly, to yourself.

- You are at a job interview and you are asked what you think about a certain aspect of the job you are applying for. Answering "I like it" or "I do not like it" will not do. You will be expected to give details and to **express yourself clearly and coherently**.

- In 2009, the world was faced with the H1N1 pandemic. In response to this situation, the Canadian government went on a massive vaccination campaign. So many things were said about this flu shot in the media. Who and what should you believe? Was it really safe? Did the risk outweigh the potential cost?

As you can see, critical thinking is used every day in all aspects of your life. It will help you evaluate the information that is given to you and form an educated opinion, which you will then be able to back up on clear and coherent grounds. It will enable you to justify your belief to others and sometimes even convince them that your view is the correct one. What's more, critical thinking skills will help you in your decision making process and reassure you that you made the best decision possible, especially when faced with difficult situations.

Chapter 2

ARGUMENT

How to recognize an argument

One of the main components of critical thinking is the ability to evaluate and create arguments. Hence, this will be our starting point. We will start by defining arguments in terms of structure: what do they look like; what are the components needed. Once the structure of an argument is understood, we will look at the quality of an argument.

An **argument** is a set of premises[1] that lead to a conclusion. You need at least one premise that leads to a conclusion to have an argument. Both elements, premise and conclusion, are needed. In laymen's terms, an argument is a series of sentences that attempt to show that something is necessarily true. It is a succession of reasons that support a conclusion. An argument can be as long or as short as desired or needed. As long as there is at least one premise and one conclusion and as long as the premises support the conclusion, you have an argument.

---

[1] A **premise** is a sentence that provides a **reason** as to why the conclusion is true.

Example 1:

1. *Killing innocent people is always wrong*
2. *Euthanasia is the killing of innocent people* } premises

---

3. *Therefore, euthanasia is wrong* } *conclusion*

In this example, lines 1 and 2 are giving reasons as to why euthanasia is wrong. They are the premises of the argument. Line 3 is the claim being defended by the premises and is thus the conclusion.

In this example, the argument is clearly spelled out. Each premise has its own line, is numbered and the conclusion starts with an obvious conclusion indicator: the word '*therefore*'. Writing an argument in this way is called **standardizing** it. Standardizing an argument makes it easier for you to follow its logical structure and hence to analyze it. However, when you are reading a text or essay, this is not how it will appear. In the next section, you will learn how to recognize an argument and write it in its standardized form.

How to find an argument

Recognizing an argument within an essay is probably the most valuable skill that you can learn as a student. Being able to decipher an argument will enable you to better understand what an author is saying. More importantly, combined with critical thinking skills, being capable of recognizing an argument will enable you to give appropriate response, in depth analysis as well as significant criticism of the information given in a text.

To be able to find an argument, you must first read the text and try to understand it. You should try to identify the conclusion first and then look for the premises. There are many "tricks" that can help you achieve this. Consider the following example:

Example 2

There is more violence on TV today than there was 20 years ago. ***Because*** *there is more violence on TV, and* ***given that*** *children are more violent today than 20 years ago,* ***it follows*** *that violence on TV causes children to be more violent.*

This can be rewritten in the following form:

1. *There is more violence on TV today than there was 20 years ago*
2. *Children are more violent today than 20 years ago*
3. ***Therefore****, violence on TV causes children to be more violent*

Whether this is a good argument or not is not important at this point. We are only using this example to better understand the structure of an argument and its different components.

Certain words in the paragraph served as clues to help distinguish the premises from the conclusion. The word "**because**" usually indicates that a reason is about to be given. Hence, there is a good chance that the sentence in which it appears is a premise. The words "**given that**" also usually tend to mean that a reason is about to follow. Again, one can assume that the sentence in which it appears is also a premise. The words "**it follows that**" typically indicate the presence of a conclusion. Such words are called **indicator words. Indicator words** can sometimes help you identify premises and conclusions. Unfortunately, while using indicator words can help you find premises and a conclusion in a text, they are no guarantees. The presence of an indicator word does not necessarily mean that the sentence is a premise or a conclusion. However, if you are having a hard time understanding the meaning of the text, indicator words can give you a starting point for your analysis.

The structure of the above argument was somewhat easy to identify: the premises are presented one after the other and are followed directly by the conclusion. There are no additional sentences present to stray us from the argument. Furthermore, there are obvious indicator words. Evidently, this is not always the case (actually, it is rarely the case).

Here is an argument that is a little more complex to identify:

Example 3

"Many of you would like to do well in school. Taking a study skills course could help you achieve this goal. A study skills course is designed to give you information on how to improve your skills as a student, in the hopes of improving your grade point average. However, it is a mistake to think that your grades will improve solely by attending such a class. A class cannot monitor your behaviour and ensure that you are actually applying what you have learned. Listening is not sufficient. Knowledge about how to get good grades will not produce good grades. Getting good grades involves applying that knowledge."

In this example, the conclusion is stated before the premises. The other sentences serve to support the first sentence. Standardized, the argument looks like this:

1. *A study skills course provides knowledge on how to get good grades*
2. *Getting good grades is not purely based on gaining knowledge on how to get good grades*
3. *Getting good grades involves applying the knowledge gained on how to get good grades*
4. *A study skills course cannot ensure that you are applying the course content*

---

5. *Therefore, getting good grades cannot be achieved solely by attending a study skills course*

As you can see, one had to understand the meaning of the information in order to be able to write the argument in standardized form. Nevertheless, the more familiar you are with indicator words (and their synonyms), the easier recognizing arguments and standardizing them will be. Here is a list of the most common premise and conclusion indicators:

PREMISE INDICATORS

Since	Because
If	May be derived from
Follows from	As shown by
Given that	Seeing as
On account of	On the grounds that
Inasmuch as	For the reason that
As indicated by	May be inferred from
For	May be deduced from

CONCLUSION INDICATORS

Therefore	Indicates that
Thus	We can conclude that
So	We can infer that
Hence	Demonstrates that
Then	Proves that
Shows that	It follows that
In conclusion	It can be inferred that
Accordingly	Consequently
As a result	On these grounds it is clear that
For this reason	

Not an argument

It is important to realize that indicator words can serve as clues, but they do not guarantee the presence of an argument. There are many different kinds of ways of conveying different kinds of information. Arguments are not always present in what you hear or read. Consider the following examples:

Example 4

> *"In 1889, the famous chef Raffaele Esposito created a special pizza in honour of Queen Margherita of Italy. The white cheese, red tomato sauce, and green herbs matched the colors of the Italian flag. This creation was named 'pizza all Margherita' after her."*

In this paragraph, there is no argument. We are only exposed to a **series of facts** and **no conclusion is being defended**. Although facts are needed to build premises, unless there is a conclusion to which all these facts relate, what is presented cannot be an argument. A series of facts does not constitute an argument.

Example 5

> *"I don't like Halloween. I think it's a stupid holiday. To me, having to dress up in silly costumes is ridiculous."*

These sentences are only expressing **emotions**. No argument is given here. Emotions never justify a conclusion. They cannot serve as premises nor should they be of any value for good critical thinking skills. The same is true of opinions. Although the conclusion of your argument can reflect your opinion, **opinions cannot serve as premises**. For example, if I say that homosexuality is wrong because when I see two guys kissing it grosses me out then I would have to be justified in saying that open heart surgery or giving birth is wrong because it grosses me out. The flaw in using emotions as means of justification is more obvious in the latter however, it is equally wrong in both cases.

Example 6

"Don't you think abortion should be legal? Do you know that the fetus cannot reason as humans do? Shouldn't women be in control of their bodies? Wouldn't you want to be able to have the choice if it was you?"

These sentences raise many questions on the issue of abortion, but offer no argument. **Questions** are never good arguing tools nor can they serve as premises. In the above example, the writer expects the reader to answer 'yes' to all questions. However, there is no guarantee that this will be the case. One could easily answer 'no' or even 'I don't know' to any or all of these questions. Writers should never assume that readers will answer 'yes' simply because that is what they believe. That is why when you write, you should always turn your questions into clear statements and support them with proper justification. If you want your reader to think that the fetus is not a person, then you should assert that the fetus is not a person and give your various reasons as to why this should be taken to be true.

Example 7

> *"Santa Claus wears a red suit trimmed with white fur, big black boots, a belt, and a hat. He has a white beard and he is a big, jolly man. He travels in a sleigh pulled by eight flying reindeers."*

Again, this is not an argument. This is nothing more than a description of a specific person. **Descriptions in themselves do not justify a conclusion**.

Example 8

> *"Smoking cigarettes is not something that interests me. Because my mother smoked, she died of lung cancer. I also became asthmatic as a result of all the second hand smoke. I do not want my teeth to get yellow nor am I interested in the bad breath that is associated with smoking. That is why I will never be a smoker."*

This passage is a little trickier because it contains indicator words such as 'because' and 'that is why'. However, it is not an argument. We are not trying to convince the reader of anything. Rather, this is an **explanation**. The person who wrote this is simply trying to explain to readers why he feels the way he does, as opposed to convincing them that that is how he felt or that it is how everybody should feel. There is a fine line between an explanation and an argument and with practice you will be able to see it. In the next example, the fictitious information is reworded to produce an argument (again, this does not mean that it is a good argument. The example provides sentences that have the structure of an argument).

Example 9

"People should not smoke cigarettes. A study showed that smoking increases your chances of developing lung and throat cancer. Since second hand smoke was also shown to have detrimental effects, smoking is not respectful of others. In addition, smoking is bad for dental hygiene and creates unpleasant odors for others. That is why people should not smoke cigarettes."

ACTIVITY 1

Read the following passages and determine whether they are arguments or not. If the passage is an argument, write it in its standardized form. If it is not an argument, then identify what it is.

1. When I was twenty-five, I lived in the Dominican Republic for six months. This Latin country only has one neighbour: Haiti. Seeing as these two countries are surrounded by water and share the same island, it seems reasonable for me to say that I lived on an island for six months.

2. 'Hamster' is an English word that is derived from an old German verb, 'hamste', which means "to hoard or put away for use later on". And this, of course, is just what hamsters do. They store food in their mouths and move it from one place to the next until it is time to use it.

3. Ever since I was six, I have been afraid of spiders. I remember seeing a movie where people would get bitten by one and die. Today, I know that this is not true of spiders and that most of them are inoffensive, but I still remember the movie and I am still afraid of spiders.

4. I do not believe in abortion. It is a disgusting, sickening and unspeakable action.

5. Since I am taller than my sister and my sister is taller than my brother, then I am taller than my brother.

6. On a beautiful Sunday morning, I woke up on the sandy beaches of a little mountain lake somewhere in the Canadian Rockies. As the sun was dancing on my face, the warm sand was running through my toes. All of nature's instruments came together and created a symphony of joy and inner peace.

7. 15% of American children between the ages of 6 and 19 are overweight. The US Center for Disease Control and Prevention says that this figure is four times what is was 40 years ago. Medical costs for overweight kids in the US have tripled to 127 million$. In Canada, 33% of boys and more than 25% of girls are overweight.

8. All non-francophone students should try to go to Quebec City on a regular basis. First, their French will improve. Second, they will learn more about Quebecois culture. Third, they will improve their understanding of the political situation in Quebec.

9. I went to Quebec City for the winter holidays and stayed with a Quebecois family. My French improved dramatically, I learned more about Quebecois culture, and I improved my understanding of the political situation in Quebec.

Chapter 2 exercises

Read the following passages and determine whether they are arguments or not. If the passage is an argument, write it in its standardized form. If it is not an argument, then identify what it is.

1. Don't you think that Plato's theories on rationalism are true? Did you know that he was Aristotle's teacher? Don't you think he was a great philosopher?
2. There is a mysterious quality to Pre-Socratic thought. The original context of their writing is lost. All we have are cryptic passages that stimulate the imagination.
3. Since we do not know the original context of the writings and seeing as we only have passages and not complete works, it is thus very difficult to be certain of the actual intentions of Pre-Socratic philosophers.
4. Aristotle's works are simply fascinating. Upon reading them, one cannot help but feel delight, bliss and ecstasy. His works are simply pure joy.
5. When I first started reading my ancient world textbook, I did not understand anything. This is because I was not used to the writing style and the terminology employed. I was also not accustomed to reading so many pages at once.
6. The decisive shift toward modern art came in 1914 with the beginning of World War 1. Expressionism was rooted in Gothic and Romantic art and influenced by van Gogh and Matisse. This form of art was shaped by the desire to liberate color from the constraints of the natural world with dramatic simplification.
7. Claude Monet's "*Water Lilies*" is simply magnificent. It is a painting that makes one feel powerful vastness. It is of obvious overwhelming importance.
8. Do you know why Michael Jackson was considered the king of pop? Did you know that he was the lead singer of the Jackson 5 and that his T*hriller* album remains the best-selling album ever? Did you know that he popularized a number of complicated dance techniques (like the robot and the moonwalk)? How many other pop singers transcended generational, racial and cultural barriers?

9. The YMCA dance starts by standing straight with your legs together and arms above your head. Arms should be exactly 89 cm apart. After holding this position for 1.8 seconds, bring back of hands together and lower them 11 cm over your head. Quickly separate hands and simultaneously bring right bicep to right ear and left elbow onto left hip (while keeping arms in arch position). Then while jumping to separate legs (about 49 cm) quickly straighten arms and bring palms together above your head.
10. Michael Jackson is considered the king of pop for several reasons. For starters, his *Thriller* album remains the best-selling album ever. Also, he popularized a number of complicated dance techniques (like the robot and the moonwalk). He is the only pop singer that transcended generational, racial and cultural barriers.
11. In 2005 it was estimated that there were about 1 282 780 149 Muslims, 856 690 863 Hindus and 381 610 979 Buddhists. Hence, with an estimated total of 2 116 909 552 adherents, it is clear that Christianity is the most popular religion in the world.
12. Did you know that Buddhism is a great religion? Did you know that Buddha did not see himself as a God? How can one not appreciate his teachings of wisdom and compassion that are to be grasped through meditation?
13. In 2005 it was estimated that there were about 2 116 909 552 Christians in the world (including Roman Catholics, Protestants, Orthodox and Anglicans). They were to be followed by an estimated 1 282 780 149 Muslims, 856 690 863 Hindus and 381 610 979 Buddhists.
14. Because I have never seen God, nor have I witnessed a miracle and because some of the writings in the Bible make no sense, I do not believe that there is such a thing as a God.
15. Ganesha is one of many Hindu Gods. Easy to recognize with his elephant head, he rides a rat while carrying a conch. He can also be seen with snakes, a hatchet and a broken tusk.
16. The solar system is comprised of eight planets. The closest one to the sun is Mercury followed by Venus, Earth, Mars, Jupiter, Saturn, Uranus and Neptune. Pluto is no longer considered a planet (but is still Mickey Mouse's Dog).

17. Doesn't it make more sense to believe in the Big Bang theory? Don't physicists have rational and scientific explanations as to how it happened? Hasn't Darwin provided a believable account of evolution? How much more proof do you need?
18. True fruits are developed from the ovary in the base of the flower. They contain the seeds of the plant. Accordingly a tomato is a fruit as it develops from the ovaries of the plant and it contains seeds.
19. I have always had a true love of science. I think it is because my dad spent hours playing chess with me, which developed my sense of logic. He would always have wacky science experiments for me to do, like the Mentos in Cola one. That is why I became a food biologist. I wanted to understand why Mentos and Cola did not create the same explosive phenomenon in a human stomach.
20. Born in 1867, Marie Curie was a physicist and chemist of Polish upbringing. She was a pioneer in the field of radioactivity, the first person honored with two Nobel Prizes (one in physics and later, one in chemistry).
21. I never believe anything I read in the newspaper. The reason is that depending on which one you read, they will have a different version of the same event.
22. The Avatar movie was quite boring. It was tedious to watch and quite dull. Nothing but a big disappointment. Simply uninteresting!
23. In 1778, Fleury Mesplet, founded the French-language newspaper called *La Gazette du commerce et littéraire, pour la ville et district de Montréal*. This paper was shut down in 1779. In 1785, Mesplet began a second weekly: *La Gazette de Montréal*. This version slowly evolved from French, to French and English to become the English-only newspaper we know today.
24. Did you know that anybody can post a website? Did you know that server providers are not responsible for content? So why should you believe anything that you find on the Internet?
25. There are more sexually explicit scenes on TV today than there were 40 years ago. Because there are more sexually explicit scenes and given that today's children are sexually active at a much younger age, it is clear that television is responsible for our youth's promiscuity.

Chapter 3

DEDUCTIVE LOGIC

There are two kinds of logic that will be discussed in this book: deductive and inductive. Once one has a good understanding of deductive logic, inductive reasoning becomes easier to understand. Although both deal with the quality of the relationship between the premises and the conclusion, deductive logic will be concerned specifically with what is called validity and soundness.

Validity

So far, we have learned what an argument is and what it is not. However, having an argument does not mean that you have good reasoning. Remember that the purpose of an argument is to show that the conclusion is true. Consider the following example:

Example 10

1. *Jessica is wearing a pink shirt*
2. *Catherine is wearing a pink shirt*
3. *Charles is wearing a pink shirt*

Therefore, there are at least four people wearing a pink shirt

In this example, it is clear that the premises do not support the conclusion. Only three people are mentioned and yet the conclusion states that at least four people are wearing a pink shirt. The premises by themselves do not show the conclusion to be necessarily true. In such a case, we will say that the truth is not preserved from the premises to the conclusion. Hence, the first criterion for a good argument would be to say that the truth must be preserved from the premises to the conclusion. When an argument is truth preserving, we say that it is **valid**. When we say that an argument is valid, it means that **it is impossible for the conclusion to be false if the premises are true**. Another way to formulate this definition would be to say: "If the premises are true, then the conclusion is necessarily true as well."

I would like to focus your attention on the word **"IF"**. This does not entail that the premises must actually be true. "IF" entails a conditional. All it means is that **IF** the premises were true, then the conclusion would also be true. Validity is about **logical structure** as opposed to truth. Something can be perfectly logical yet false.

Here is an **example of a valid argument**:

Example 11

1. *Jessica is wearing a pink shirt*
2. *Catherine is wearing a pink shirt*
3. *Charles is wearing a pink shirt*

Therefore, there are at least three people wearing a pink shirt

In this argument, the truth is preserved from the premises to the conclusion. If Jessica, Catherine and Charles are in fact wearing pink shirts, then it follows (or it must be true) that there are at least three people wearing a pink shirt. Whether Jessica, Catherine and Charles are actually wearing a pink

shirt or not is of no importance for validity. We are only concerned with the hypothesis of IF they are wearing a pink shirt. Validity merely assesses the logical connection between the premises and the conclusion.

Here is an **example of an argument that is not valid** (invalid):

Example 12

1. *Jessica is wearing a pink shirt*
2. *Catherine is wearing a pink shirt*
3. *Charles is wearing a pink shirt*

Therefore, everyone is wearing a pink shirt

As with our first example, information is given on three people only. One cannot conclude from this that "everyone" is wearing a pink shirt. There could be other people besides these three and thus, we could not know if everyone is wearing a pink shirt. You must be careful of words such as 'everyone', 'none', 'some', 'never', 'always', 'many', etc. They carry specific meanings that can have consequences on the logical structure of statements.

Here is another **example of an invalid argument**:

Example 13

1. *Montreal is in Quebec*
2. *Calgary is in Alberta.*
3. *Winnipeg is in Manitoba*

Therefore, Vancouver is in Ontario

In this case, we know that all the premises are true. However, we also know that the conclusion is false. Because a conclusion cannot be false when its premises are true, this argument is invalid. More importantly, there is absolutely no connection between the premises and the conclusion. Knowing where Montreal, Calgary and Winnipeg are does not help you know in any way where Vancouver is.

Here is another **example of an invalid argument**:

Example 14

1. *Montreal is in the province of Quebec*
2. *Calgary is in the province of Alberta.*
3. *Winnipeg is in the province of Manitoba*

Therefore, Vancouver is in the province of British Columbia

In this case, some are tempted to say that the argument is valid. But it is not. We know that the premises are true, and we know that the conclusion is true. However, the conclusion is not true because the premises support it. We know the conclusion to be true because of common knowledge. Hence, it could be the case that someone will change the name of the city of Vancouver to something else or that BC will separate and become its own country. These are two plausible hypotheses. This means that it could be possible for the premises to be true and the conclusion false. I will grant that this is somewhat farfetched, but the idea to retain is that there needs to be some kind of link between the premises and the conclusion; the premises must be self-sufficient in supporting the conclusion if we are to have a good argument. As with the previous example, there is no relationship between the premises and the conclusion. This example also illustrates that 'true premises' does not necessarily mean 'good argument'.

Here is another **example of an invalid argument**:

Example 15

1. *All teenagers listen to music on Mp3 players*
2. *Tom is listening to music on an Mp3 player*

Therefore, Tom is a teenager.

In this example, although Tom is listening to music on an Mp3 player, it does not necessarily mean that he is a teenager. The premise does not say that only teenagers listen to Mp3 players Tom could be an adult too. . If this possibility is not clear to you, consider the following diagram:

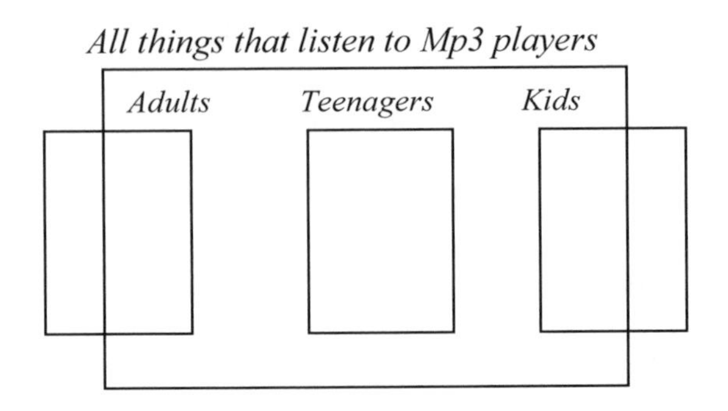

From the diagram, it is clear that all teenagers listen to Mp3 players, but it is also clear that there are other beings that can listen to Mp3 players. Saying that all teenagers listen to music on Mp3 players does not mean that they are the only ones that can do so. According to the information given in the argument, Tom could be an adult, child or teenager. Since we are not certain, then the argument cannot be valid. **For an argument to be valid the conclusion must be more than possible; it must be certain.**

The last example is to be contrasted with the following:

Example 16

1. *All teenagers listen to music on Mp3 players*
2. *Tom is a teenager*

---

3. *Therefore, Tom listens to music on an Mp3 player.*

This argument would yield the following diagram:

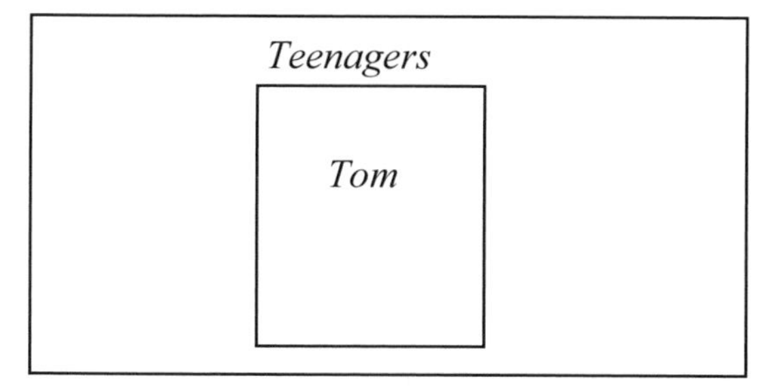

From the diagram, it is clearer that the logic is preserved from the premises to the conclusion and that if the premises are true, the conclusion is certain to be true as well. Hence, the argument is valid. Whenever in doubt, taking the time to draw out a little diagram will help you understand the relationship between the different claims being made and the conclusion.

Now that you have learned to identify valid and invalid arguments, the next step is to verify their soundness.

Soundness

Validity tells us that if the premises are true, then the conclusion must also be true. However, validity, by itself, does not assure a good argument. Consider the example already given:

Example 17

1. *Jessica is wearing a pink shirt*
2. *Catherine is wearing a pink shirt*
3. *Charles is wearing a pink shirt*

Therefore, there are at least three people wearing a pink shirt

For validity, we operated on the HYPOTHESIS or the ASSUMPTION that the premises were true. But are they true? Is Jessica wearing a pink shirt? This sentence could be true but it could also be false. She could be wearing a green shirt. If we have very good reasons to believe that Jessica, Catherine and Charles are wearing pink shirts, then we know that the conclusion must be true.

When a valid argument's premises are all true, then this argument is said to be **sound**. Thus, **an argument is sound if and only if, it is valid <u>and</u> all of its premises are actually true**.

Here is an **example of a sound argument**:

Example 18

1. *A rectangle is defined as a shape that has four sides and four 90° angles.*
2. *A square is defined as a shape that has four equal sides and four 90° angles.*

---

3. *Therefore, a square is a rectangle.*

In this example, we know that the argument is at least valid. That is to say, it is impossible for the premises to be true and the conclusion to be false at the same time. Since we know the premises are in fact true, then the argument is also sound.

Here is an **example of an argument that is valid, but not sound**:

Example 19

1. *Toronto is the capital of Canada*
2. *The capital of Canada is in Ontario*

Therefore, Toronto is in Ontario

In this example, if the premises were true, the conclusion would also have to be true and thus, the argument is valid. However, the first premise of the argument is false. Toronto is not the capital of Canada; Ottawa is. Because one of the premises is false, this argument is not sound. This also illustrates that you can have good reasoning, end up with a true conclusion while your premises are false. This is why soundness is important. It ensures that you have good reasoning **and** that what you are saying is also true.

Here is an **example of an argument that has true premises but that is not sound:**

Example 20

1. *Montreal is in the province of Quebec*
2. *Toronto is in the province of Ontario*

---

3. *Therefore, Vancouver is in the Province of British Columbia*

In this example, all premises are true. However, as it was discussed before, the argument is not valid. The premises do not support the conclusion. Since the argument is not valid, it cannot be sound. The point of this example is to show you why a sound argument needs to be valid and cannot only rely on truth. It also serves to remind you that logic and truth are two very different concepts and that both are important in assessing the quality of an argument.

Ultimately, all arguments should strive at being sound. A claim defended by a sound argument is true for everyone, everywhere, at all times. It becomes a **universal truth**; one that is not refutable. Needless to say that a sound argument is the best argument one can come up with. If you have proven something with a sound argument, no one will ever be able to refute it.

ACTIVITY 2

Cut out the boxes following the dotted lines and shuffle the sentences to create arguments that are at least valid and then arguments that are sound

Is abortion the killing of an innocent baby?	Sonia has four legs, a mouth and a nose.
A cat can fly.	Everyone has a radio.
I am.	Is the fetus deserving of rights?
A cat can be blue.	Many people have a radio.
Sonia is a cat.	Is the fetus a human being?
Do you think?	It is possible to hear music on the radio.
I think.	This is the best game any Humanities teacher ever made me play.
Many people can listen to music.	All blue animals can fly.
A cat can eat and drink.	'Cat' is a three-letter word.
A cat is an animal.	Everyone can listen to music.
A cat has four legs, a mouth and a nose.	A cat can be black, white or brown.
Abortion should be illegal.	What am I supposed to do exactly?

Chapter 3 exercises

Read the following arguments and determine
a) if the argument is valid,
b) if the premises are true and
c) if the argument is sound.

1. -Socrates was a famous philosopher
   -Socrates was a man
   -Therefore, all men are famous philosophers
2. -Many people used to live in Ancient Greece
   -Greek mythology is still the system of belief used by Greeks today
   -Therefore, Greek mythology provides the truth as to the origins of things.
3. -Socrates was a man that lived in Ancient Greece
   -All men that lived in Ancient Greece were philosophers
   -Therefore, Socrates was a philosopher
4. -Greek Mythology was based on faith and not reason
   -Science is a system of belief that is based on reason
   -Therefore, Greek Mythology is not a science
5. -Plato received philosophical lessons from Socrates
   -One who gives lessons can be called a teacher
   -Therefore, one could say that Socrates was a philosophy teacher
6. -Michael Jackson was a famous singer
   -Michael Jackson was an American
   -Therefore, America gave rise to at least one famous singer
7. -Pablo Picasso was a famous painter
   -Pablo Picasso was born in China
   -Therefore, China gave rise to at least one famous painter
8. -The original *Mona Lisa* is exposed in The *Louvre* museum
   -The *Louvre* museum is located in France
   -Therefore, the original *Mona Lisa* is in France

9. -Salsa is a type of dance that comes from Latin America
   -Dance is a form of art
   -Therefore all Latin Americans are artists
10. -Elvis Presley songs still play on the radio today
    -Every night, Elvis Presley appears in movies on television
    -Therefore, Elvis Presley is still alive
11. -Religious beliefs are based on faith
    -Faith implies that there is no scientific justification for the belief
    -Therefore, Religious beliefs do not have scientific justifications to support them
12. –Hinduism is a religious belief held by many in the world
    -Christianity is a religious belief held by many in the world
    -Buddhism is a religious belief held by many in the world
    -Therefore, there are several different religious beliefs in the world
13. -To pray properly, one must be in a noisy and chaotic area
    -Patrick is at the Black and Blue rave right now
    -Therefore, Patrick is praying
14. -The bible says that it is the written word of God
    -God does not lie
    -Therefore, the bible is the written word of God
15. -All Muslims are terrorists
    -Abdul is a terrorist
    -Therefore, Abdul is a Muslim
16. -Water freezes at 0°C
    -The temperature is always below 0°C in Mexico
    -There is no way to heat water in Mexico
    -Therefore, the water in Mexico is frozen
17. -A triangle has three sides
    -A square has four sides
    -Therefore a pentagon has five sides
18. -True fruits are developed from the ovary in the base of the flower of a plant
    -True fruits contain the seeds of the plant
    -Tomatoes develop from the ovaries of the plant and contain the seeds
    -Therefore, tomatoes are a fruit

19. -Physics is a science that is studied in Canadian universities
    -Chemistry is a science that is studied in Canadian universities
    -Prostitution is studied in Canadian universities
    -Therefore prostitution is a science
20. -The human body is made of organs
    -Organs are made of cells
    -Therefore, the human body is made of cells
21. -The Gazette is an English Newspaper in Montreal
    -Montreal is in the province of Quebec
    -Therefore, there is at least one English newspaper in the province of Quebec
22. -Kids imitate everything they see on TV
    -There is violence on TV
    -Kids see violence on TV
    -TV creates violent behaviour in kids
23. -Only highly intelligent people know how to use the Internet
    -Virginia is highly intelligent
    -Therefore, Virginia knows how to use the Internet
24. -Several books state that Santa Clause exists
    -Therefore, Santa Clause exists
25. -Up until January 20th 2009, all American presidents were white
    -Barack Obama became the president of the United States on January 20th 2009 (even though he won the elections in November 2008)
    -Barack Obama is black
    -Therefore Barack Obama is the first black president of the United States

Chapter 4

INDUCTIVE ARGUMENTS

Difference between inductive and deductive logic

So far, we have been focusing on **deductive** arguments: arguments that can be evaluated in terms of validity and soundness. However, there are good arguments that are not deductively valid. Consider the following argument:

Example 21

1. *Children who play violent video games display violent behaviours when playing with their friends.*
2. *Children who do not play violent video games do not display violent behaviours when playing with their friends.*
3. *Therefore, violent video games cause children to be more violent.*

This argument is not deductively valid. These observations could all be coincidental. For example, it could be that the children who play the violent video games were violent beforehand and that is why they were attracted to the violent games to begin with. The point is that from the premises, the conclusion is not certain. However, the conclusion that violent video games cause children to be more violent is probable.

As you know, an argument that is not valid cannot be sound. However, an argument that is not deductively valid can still be useful. The premises can **make the conclusion likely even**

though not certain. In these situations, we will turn to **inductive** logic; we will talk about ***inductive strength***.

An argument will be qualified as ***inductively strong or inductively weak*** depending on the degree of probability that the premises lead to the conclusion and on how acceptable the premises are. The objective is to have a good logical connection between the premises and the conclusion and to have premises that are strong enough to be considered true. Inductive arguments are not as clear- or straightforward to analyze as deductive ones. There is more room for interpretation and discussion when analyzing inductive arguments and more will be said on this topic in the 'analyzing a thesis essay' section of this book. Of course, if the inductive argument contains a false premise, then it is automatically inductively weak. In the example given above, although the argument has no deductive worth (because it is invalid and not sound) the argument can be said to be inductively interesting.

Here is another example of an inductive argument:

Example 22

1. *Bob's first computer was a PC*
2. *In the last 5 years, Bob has always owned a PC*
3. *Therefore, the next computer that Bob will buy will be a PC*

In this example, although the conclusion seems plausible, it is not certain. It could be the case that Bob will buy a Mac or that a new kind of computer will come into existence. In this particular argument, even if the premises were all true, because they are somewhat vague, they render the conclusion plausible, but not highly likely. For instance, from the premises, we do not know if Bob has owned the same PC for five years or perhaps he did not have enough money to buy another computer and still owns his first PC. Hence, we would **not** say that this is an inductively strong argument because the connection between the premises and the conclusion is not very good.

How do I know whether to use deductive or inductive logic?

Whether to use deductive or inductive logic depends on the context. If an argument is given with the assumption that if the premises are true, the **conclusion must also be true**, then the argument should be evaluated by the standards of **deductive** logic (validity and soundness). On the other hand, if an argument is given with the weaker assumption that if the premises are true the **conclusion is probable**, then the argument should be evaluated by the standards of **inductive** logic (inductively weak or inductively strong).

Inductive logic relies on frequency of occurrence. Because a certain phenomenon has been seen to occur several times, one will induce that it must always be the case. To use Bertrand Russell's example, how do you know that the sun will rise tomorrow? Most of you will answer, well it came up yesterday, the day before yesterday, last week, last year actually, for the last 4 billion years, and hence there is no reason to think that the sun will not rise tomorrow. Because the phenomenon of the sun rising in the morning has occurred so many times in the past, you can induce that the sun will also rise tomorrow. However, it is not a certainty that the sun will rise tomorrow. It is only highly probable. One could imagine that an asteroid will collide with the earth and that the earth will explode and hence, the sun would not rise tomorrow. All arguments that are based on observations and frequency of occurrence are inductive arguments.

Deductive logic is not based on observations. **Deductions are based on derivations of definitions**. For example, how do you know that '1+1=2'? Is it because you observed that every time you have a '1' and another '1', in effect you have two? Or is it because the number '2' has been defined as meaning '1+1'? As you can see, the number '2' is defined as being

'1+1'. It has nothing to do with frequency of occurrence. The same goes for the number '4'. '4' is defined as being '1+1+1+1'. By "playing" with the definition of '1+1' and the definition of the number '4', we arrive at a new equation of '2+2=4'. You did not need to observe anything in the real world. You simply needed to move the various definitions around:

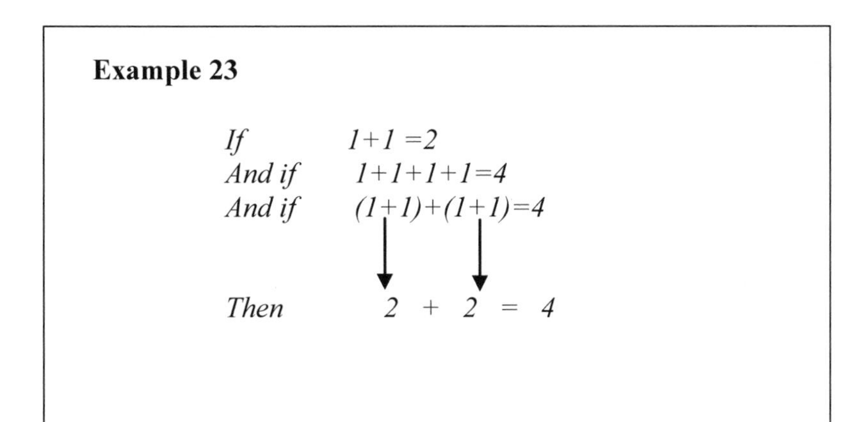

ACTIVITY 3

Read the following passages and determine whether they are examples of inductive or deductive logic.

a) There is more violence on TV today than there was 20 years ago.
Children are more violent today than 20 years ago.
Therefore, violence on TV causes children to be more violent.

b) Jessica is a vegetarian.
Catherine is a vegetarian
Charles is a vegetarian.
Therefore, there are at least three vegetarians.

c) After conducting an experiment, it was shown that 77% of rats that were exposed to RCL cleaning products developed a form of skin cancer. Hence, it is clear that RCL cleaning products should not be sold to the general public as it can cause skin cancer.

d) Every Tuesday for the past 8 years, Tom and Jane have gone to the movies together. Today is Tuesday. It seems safe to say that Tom and Jane will see a movie today.

e) An 8 Go Mp3 player costs about 100$ while a 16 Go Mp3 player is about 150$. Hence it is cheaper in the long run to by a 16 Go Mp3 player as two 8 Go players would cost 200$.

f) You have been in school since you have been five years old. You have learned to read and to count, which shows that you are teachable. You have passed all classes needed to earn your high school diploma. You have shown yourself capable of learning several different things and succeed. Therefore, there is no reason to think that you will not succeed at this as well.

Chapter 4 exercises

Read the following passages and determine whether they are examples of inductive or deductive logic.

1. Socrates was a man and since all men are mortal, Socrates was mortal.
2. Thales was known to love stargazing. He spent many nights observing the stars. A servant girl claims to have seen and mocked Thales for falling into a well while he was stargazing. Considering the amount of time he spent looking at the stars, it is hard to believe that it only happened once and that she is the only one who saw him.
3. Anaximander was born in Miletus in 610 B.C.E., which was part of Greece at the time. Hence, Anaximander was Greek.
4. Anaximander says that in the beginning man was born from creatures of a different kind. He concludes this after observing that other creatures are all self-supporting soon after birth. Man is the only one that needs prolonged nursing.
5. Since Antiquity comes before the medieval times and that the medieval times come before the Renaissance, it is clear that Antiquity comes before the Renaissance.
6. Since all of Celine Dion's CDs were hits, her next one will be one too.
7. Since all of Picasso's paintings are worth a lot of money, if a new one was to be discovered today, it would be worth a lot of money too.
8. To be part of the Grand Ballet Canadien's dance crew, one has to have received formal training in classical ballet. Bill is part of the Grand Ballet Canadien's dance crew, so he has formal training in classical ballet.
9. A sculpture is a three dimensional form of art. *The Thinker* by Rodin is a famous piece of art and is three-dimensional; hence, it is a sculpture.
10. One paintbrush costs 4.25$ at the art store. However, if you buy a pack of five, it is only 20$ for the pack. Hence it is cheaper to buy them in packs of five as you save 0.25$ per paintbrush.

11. When I went to Egypt, everyone I spoke to was a Muslim. Hence all Egyptians are Muslims.
12. Something perfect must be whole. If two parts are needed, then it means that it is not self-sufficient, and thus not perfect. Following this logic, Since God is perfect, then he must be whole, and not part of something greater.
13. Isaak has gone to church every Sunday since he has been born. He has never missed once. So this Sunday, he will be going to church for certain.
14. Walter baptized his two first children so he is sure to baptize his third one too.
15. Since I am a practicing Jewish girl and that Judaism is a religion, it is safe to say that I am a religious person.
16. A study was done where researchers put *Pukerup* lipstick on rats for 60 consecutive days. It was found that 78% of rats developed skin cancer. Consequently, *Pukerup* lipstick should be taken off the market.
17. Newton observed that all objects fall to the ground. From this, he concluded that all objects must necessarily and always fall to the ground. Newton decided to call this phenomenon gravity.
18. Seeing as the sum of all angles in a quadrangle is 360° and that a triangle is half of a quadrangle, it is clear that the sum of all angles in a triangle will be equal to 180° (360/2).
19. Is the number of meters contained in a km based on inductive or deductive logic?
20. Is Darwin's theory of evolution based on inductive or deductive logic?
21. Is information given on the weather channel based on inductive or deductive logic?
22. Is looking for information in a phone book based on inductive or deductive logic?
23. Is choosing a radio station to listen to the #1 hit of the week (or your favorite song) based on inductive or deductive logic?
24. Is buying a newspaper because you want to read your horoscope or do the word puzzle based on inductive or deductive logic?
25. Will you use deductive or inductive logic to figure out what your yearly cost for advertising on a billboard is, considering that you know your monthly fee?

Chapter **5**

TRUTH OF A PREMISE

Whether the argument is deductive or inductive, the idea is to assess the quality of the argument. In both cases, you will need to determine whether a premise is true or not. But on what basis will you determine whether a premise is true? Here is a list of situations in which it is reasonable to accept a premise as true:

1. When the premise is supported by a good sub argument

If the arguer or someone else has already supplied a sound argument as to why we should accept this premise, then we should take it to be true.

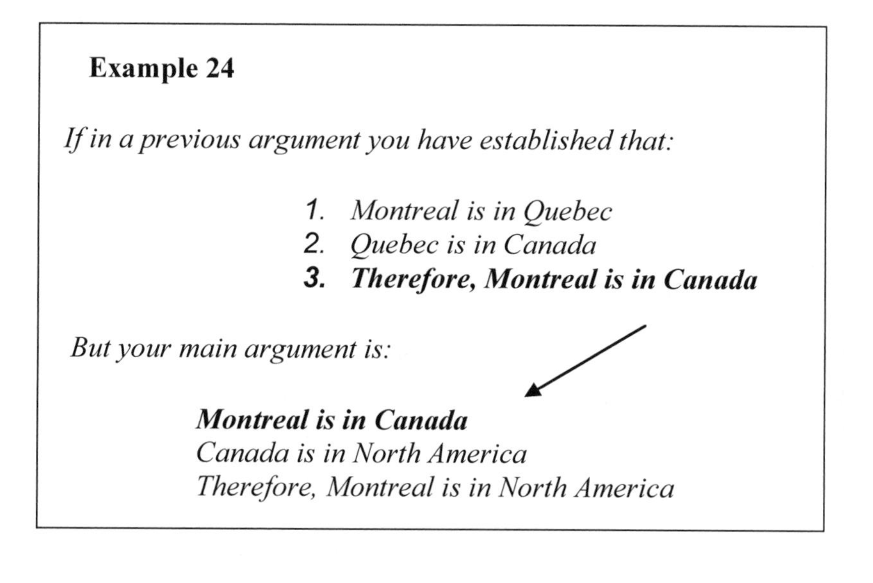

Example 24

If in a previous argument you have established that:

1. *Montreal is in Quebec*
2. *Quebec is in Canada*
3. ***Therefore, Montreal is in Canada***

But your main argument is:

Montreal is in Canada
Canada is in North America
Therefore, Montreal is in North America

You know that premise one is true because it has been established in a previous sound sub argument. Granted, in this particular example, you could have simply relied on common knowledge. This example only serves to explain the principle.

2. When the premise is known to be true *a priori*

This means that the information in the premise is independent of experience. For example, “a blind person cannot see”. In this sentence, we do not need to verify whether blind people can see or not. By the nature of the meaning of the word ‘blind’, we know *a priori* that a blind person cannot see. This is different than saying: " Pascal Bélanger is blind". To know whether it is true or not, we have to know who Pascal Bélanger is and whether he is blind or not. We will need to verify the claim and base our answer on our experience or knowledge in regards to Pascal.

3. When the premise is common knowledge

There are many claims that have become common knowledge like:

> "Cats have four legs"
>
> or
>
> "2 + 2 = 4"

Such claims should be considered as true. How do you know if something is common knowledge or not? If you think that a seventh grader living in your area would know, then it is common knowledge. For example:

> “More than 3.5 million adult Quebeckers used the Internet on a regular basis in 2004”

This claim is not common knowledge. Perhaps you know this because you recently read an article on the topic. However, a seventh grader would not know this.

Also, it should be noted that what is considered common knowledge to someone who lives in Montreal will not be the same as what is common knowledge to someone who lives in China. Common knowledge is dependent on context. I doubt that you know who the head of China is. However I am certain that you know who the mayor of Montreal is.

4. When the premise is supported by a relevant figure of authority

If an individual that is considered an expert in that field of knowledge supports a claim, then it is reasonable to think that the premise is true. For example, a statement on what causes heart disease that is given by a doctor is acceptable. However, if it is given by a restaurant owner, that is not enough grounds to accept his or her claim as true, even if it might be true.

When reading or writing an essay, all information that is not supported by a good sub argument, that is not *a priori* true or that is not common knowledge will need to be referenced. It is the reference that will enable the reader to establish whether the information is given by a relevant figure of authority.

With the increased use of the Internet to do research, one must now be even more careful as to who wrote the article in which the information is found. Anyone can have a web page on the net and they can put whatever information they want on it. That is why, as a general rule, unless the information is from a peer-reviewed[2] journal or a government site, you will have to assess the relevance of the website. For example if you go on the Toyota website to find out information on one of their cars (price or gas mileage of a particular model), then

---

[2] A peer-reviewed journal is an academic journal where a panel of experts in the field (peers) reviews the articles to ensure that they are adequate.

there is no reason not to trust the information given. However, if you go on the same website and that it claims that they have the best cars, then the information is no longer reliable (as there is an obvious bias). Each situation will be different and you will have to use your judgment.

ACTIVITY 4

Go to the following websites and determine whether you would accept the information provided by them and explain why.

1. http://en.wikipedia.org
2. http://www.prochoiceactionnetwork-canada.org/index.shtml
3. http://www.statcan.gc.ca/start-debut-eng.html
4. http://www.people.com
5. http://www.ebscohost.com
6. http://www.oprah.com
7. http://www.educause.edu
8. http://www.cbc.ca
9. http://youtube.com

Unacceptable premise

Here is list of situations in which premises should be judged unacceptable:

1. When you can find a counterexample to the premise

For example, if someone says: "No famous Canadian ever had an international music career".

You could show this to be false by saying that Céline Dion is a famous Canadian and that she has an international music career. Since you found a counter example, the premise is obviously false.

2. When you know the premise to be *a priori* false

Using the example already given, if I say that I am blind and that I can see, you will know this to be *a priori* false. *A priori* is that which is knowable without any investigation - that which we know because of the very meaning of the terms.

3. When you have contradiction between premises

Obviously, if you have one premise asserting that you are bald and the other one asserting that you have hair on your head, you know at least one of them is false. It does not matter that you do not know which one is false; all you need is one false premise for an argument not to be sound or to be weak. For example, if I wanted to buy a pair of hybrid cross country skis and the sales man tells me that they no longer sell hybrid skis as skate skis need an arch that is high off the ground to function well and classical skis work best when full weight is transferred to snow and hence, a flat arch. He goes on to explain that when doing the classical step I would not be completely satisfied (as the arch would be too high off the ground) and when skate skiing, I would not be completely satisfied either. A few minutes later, he tries to sell me a pair of classical cross-country skies and as his selling point, he promotes how this model would be great for me as the arch is high off the ground and that I could skate ski with them too.

4. When the premise is vague or ambiguous (opinions)

Sometimes, the arguer will use terms that may look like they are common knowledge, but in reality, they are highly debatable. Consider the following sentence:

"To live the good life, you need a lot of money."

In this sentence, the words "good life" and "a lot of money" would need to be defined. There can be many different versions of what one considers a "good life" and how much money that takes. Five dollars to a five year old is a lot of money but probably not so exciting for you. These kinds of sentences are nothing more than opinions and as it was discussed previously, opinions cannot be premises.

5. The premises itself would need justification

Consider the following sentence:

"Ghosts exist."

There is no room for faith or intuition in assessing an argument. Having a 'gut feeling' that something is true does not provide sufficient evidence to support a claim. This does not mean that the claim is false. It simply means that it lacks justification. We would have to assume that this claim is unacceptable until proven otherwise. The same goes for extremely controversial topics such as the existence of God and other religious claims.

ACTIVITY 5

Read the following passages and determine whether or not you would accept the information given. Justify your answer using chapter vocabulary.

1. The noise heard made no sound.

2. A good partner should be loving, kind and funny.

3. The fetus is a human being.

4. In 2009, 98% of students passed their critical thinking class.

5. Karoline claims that she can play the piano. She also claims that she does not know how to play any musical instruments.

6. Pablo Picasso was born in 1881 in Malaga (Buchholz, Bühler, Hille, Kaeppele and Stotland. (2007) *ART a world history*, Abrams; New York, p.428)

7. A musician knows how to play music.

8. There is a heaven.

9. Suzuki is one of many car dealerships.

10. No woman has ever written a critical thinking book.

Chapter 5 exercises

Read the following passages and determine whether or not you would accept the information given. Justify your answer using chapter vocabulary.

1. Ancient Greece is a civilization that lasted from the archaic period of the 8th to 6th centuries BCE to 146 BCE.
2. Socrates believed that before saying anything to anyone, it should always pass the "triple filter test": you should ensure it is true, something good and lastly, it should be useful. If it does not satisfy at least one of these conditions, then you should keep quiet. (Digital Dream Door (2009). *The Best Jokes: Socrates the Great Philosopher.* Retrieved February 20, 2010 from http://digitaldreamdoor.nusie.com /pages/quotes/best_jokes2.html)
3. Philosophy is not a very useful discipline.
4. Greek Mythology offers myths of ancient Greece.
5. There were no well-know philosophers in Antiquity.
6. François-August-René Rodin was born on November 12, 1840 in France. Two of his most famous images are The thinker (1880) and the Kiss (1886).(Auguste-Rodin. (No Date) *Encyclopedia Britannica online.* Retrieved February 20, 2010, from http:// www.britannica.com)
7. Tom Cruise, the famous actor, appeared on Oprah in May 2008 to celebrate his 25 years in film. (Oprah (2008) *Oprah goes One-on-One with Tom Cruise in a Two-Part Oprah Show Special.* Retrieved February 20, 2010 from http://www.oprah.com/pressroom/Oprah-Goes-One-on-One-with -Tom-Cruise-in-Two-Part-Special)
8. Mona Lisa is smiling on Leonardo Da Vinci's painting.
9. Whether real or fake, it is impossible to have an oil painting of the Mona Lisa. Well, except for the reproduction I have hanging on my wall.
10. Elvis Presley is still alive.

11. Hinduism is the world's third largest religion after Christianity and Islam with approximately one billion adherents, most of which live in the Republic of India.
12. All educated people are Atheists.
13. Christians believe that Jesus is God's son
14. The universe was created in seven days
15. Less than 1% of the United States prison population is atheist. This seems to suggest that atheists are less likely to commit crimes. (Gross, Joel (2010) Religion Facts. Best Online Marketing Site- Joel Gross. Retrieved February 20, 2010, from http://www.blog.joelx.com/religion-facts/627)
16. Einstein is well known for his $E=mc^2$
17. A triangle has four sides
18. Unlike what is shown in movies, a laser beam would not be visible to the naked eye in space as there would be insufficient matter in the environment to make it visible. (Vaidehi (2010) Technology Facts about the world of Technology. Scientific Facts from the Science World!--- *LASER*. Retrieved on February 20, 2010 from http://tech-fact.blogspot.com)
19. In 2007, 4 cases of tetanus were reported. Before this, there had been no reported cases since 2001. (Grunau, B. and Olson, J. (2010) An interesting presentation of pediatric tetanus. *The Journal of the Canadian Association of Emergency Physicians* 12(1) p. 70. Retrieved form Academic Search Premier database. (Accession No. 47813426))
20. The fetus is a human being.
21. Mac is a computer brand.
22. The *New York Times* is the most popular newspaper in the world.
23. *Vogue* is the only fashion magazine sold in North America.
24. The 1970s original Star Trek was a great TV show.
25. The two largest kinds of media that contain violence today are movies and television. (Mega Essays (2010). Retrieved February 20, 2010, from http://www.megaessays.com)

FALLACIES

Sometimes, the problem is not with the truth of the premise, but rather its relevance. That is to say that sometimes an argument may contain premises that look relevant but when you take a closer look, are not. An attempt is made to trick or deceive you into thinking that the argument is logical. This is called fallacious reasoning and here is a list of the most popular cases of fallacies:

1. False dilemma

This type of fallacy words the argument in such a way that it distracts you from the truth. You are presented with only two alternatives: one option that is so ludicrous that it is implausible, and the other option is the one that is argued for. This type of **argument always ignores the possibility that there are more than the two stated alternatives**.

Example 25

> *"Either you buy Scrum suds laundry detergent or your clothes will not be clean."*

This is not a real alternative. There are other laundry detergents on the market and other ways to get your clothes clean like the dry cleaner. Hence, it is a false dilemma.

2. Ignorance

The arguer using this type of fallacy bases his/her argument on the assumption **that because something is not known to be true, it must be false**. An example of this is seen in the following sentence:

Example 26

"We have no proof that God exists;, therefore, the existence of God is false."

It is not because something lacks justification that it is false. It is just unjustified. These are two different things. Thus, in such a sentence, we can neither say that God does or does not exist. It is an undetermined claim that needs justification.

3. Equivocation

A fallacy of equivocation revolves **around changing the meaning of a crucial term in the course of an argument**. The best way to assess if this fallacy is committed is to define all unknown or questionable terms that appear in an argument.

Example 27

"Joe is a two-faced liar. If he has two faces, then it is possible to have a human being with four eyes and two mouths."

In this example, "two-faced" means hypocritical, and in the second sentence, it literally means that he has two faces. This example was extremely obvious, but sometimes the nuance is trickier like using the word 'human' and defining it to mean 'capable of reason' and then to find it in another premise with the meaning of having 'the human genetic code'. This type of equivocation is often seen in arguments that deal with abortion.

4. Begging the question/circularity

Arguments based on this type of fallacy assume what they are trying to prove. **In other words, the premise's truth is dependent on the conclusion's truth**. Consequently, the reasoning is circular as in the following statement:

Example 28

> *"Whatever is heavier than air will fall to the ground, because these types of objects will not float in air."*

As you can see, this type of argument uses what it is trying to conclude as part of the explanation. Another form of this type of fallacy involves using different words or language to restate the conclusion in one of the premises.

5. Appeal to pity

This type of argument **uses pity instead of reason** to persuade you of something. For example, when students ask their teacher to grade late work by saying that they have too much work in their other courses and have full-time jobs, they are not providing the teacher with a sound argument. In reality, they hope that their teacher will feel sorry for them and that they will grant them an extension. They are resorting to pity.

6. Popularity

This type of fallacy argues for and justifies a position by pointing to the fact that:

A) It is widely held to be true;

Example 29

"After a poll was conducted, it was found that 75% of the population is against abortions and hence, abortion must be wrong."[3]

The fact that many people believe something does not make it true. 500 years ago, most believed that the earth was flat. But today, we know this to be false.

B) It is held to be true by some (usually elite) sector of the population;

Example 30

"After a poll was conducted, it was found that 75% of Harvard students are against abortions and hence, abortion must be wrong."

The fact that students attend a prestigious university like Harvard does not mean that they hold the truth on an issue like abortion.

---

[3] Examples 29 and 30 are purely fictitious and only serve to help explain the principle at hand.

C) Traditional wisdom

> **Example 31**
>
> *"If you burn yourself, you should put butter on it and it will make it better."*

Although this was a widely held belief by your great-grandmothers, it is now known to be false. Butter is actually a form of oil and adding oil to something that is burning does not make it better, it makes it worse!

7. *Ad Hominem* (attacking the person)

In this fallacy, the person is being attacked instead of arguing against the claims, arguments or theories that the person has put forward.

> **Example 32**
>
> *"Einstein was a crazy old man who was thought to be dyslexic and who had no sense of fashion whatsoever; hence his theory of relativity must be wrong."*

8. Hasty Generalization

In this type of argument, the sample used to conduct the research is so small that the inference made from it is not reliable.

Example 33

"My hair dresser is gay and my best friend's hair dresser is gay; hence all hair dressers are gay."

Obviously, the fact that two hairdressers are known to be gay does not mean that ALL hairdressers are gay. Personal observations and experiences also fall within this category. Justifying a belief on the basis that it happened to you or someone you know does not provide sufficient grounds to establish that it would happen to some or all.

9. Red Herring

This fallacious reasoning occurs when an irrelevant topic is presented to divert attention from the original issue.

Example 34

"Sunlight is a better laundry detergent than the ABC brand. Just look at the price of Sunlight detergent compared to ABC's. Sunlight is more expensive and hence will make your clothes cleaner."

The price of a laundry detergent has nothing to do with performance. There is no relationship between the two.

10. Slippery Slope

This type of fallacy is very common. It is also called the "snowball effect". It is when something is said to be wrong because of the series of possible side effects it would set off.

Example 35

> *"If Quebec separates, some of the multinationals will move to other provinces. If this is the case, many Quebeckers will lose their jobs. This will create an economic crash that will lead to a great depression, which in turn will lead to massive suicides. From this, it is clear that Quebec should not separate."*

Although some of what is said in the above example could happen, there is no certain link between events. They are merely possibilities.

Example 36

> *"If once a man indulges himself in murder,*
> *Very soon he comes to think little of robbing;*
> *And from robbing he next comes to drinking and*
> *Sabbath breaking.*
> *And from that to incivility and procrastination."* [4]

In the above example, Tomas De Quincy inverted the slippery slope to create a literary effect.

There are many other types of fallacies. However, due to the nature of this course, we will only introduce you to the most popular ones to give you an idea of what to look for when you are assessing an argument.

---

4 De Quincy, Tomas (1925). *On Murder Considered as One of the Fine Arts.* In Trudy Govier (2001). *A practical study of argument, fifth edition.* Canada: Wadsworth Thomson Learning p.341

ACTIVITY 6

Read the following passages and identify the fallacy.

1. There is no proof that a Humanities class is useful; therefore, it is a waste of time.

2. What you are saying is wrong because it is not right.

3. Students who played soccer for Champlain College last year said that their coach was the best coach ever. Hence, the Champlain College soccer coach is the best coach ever.

4. Either you stay in school or you will never make money.

5. Janice gave me a hand to get the tutoring project started. This means that Janice only has one hand left.

6. I had so much grading to do that I did not get any time off during the Christmas holidays. Also, I have been working three jobs for the last six months. Furthermore, I just turned 30 and I feel old and fat. Hence, I should be allowed to take two sick days to make my spring break longer so that I can go to the Grand Canyon.

7. If you do not smoke cigarettes, you will not be cool.

8. You should never smoke pot because if you try it, you will get addicted and then you will need to resort to something stronger to get your fix. Stronger drugs are more expensive and because you will get more and more addicted, you will need more drugs and hence more money. Soon you will end up on the street because you could not pay your other bills and you will need to start stealing or resort to prostitution to pay for your drugs.

9. No one has ever come back from the dead to tell us if there is life after death; hence, it is impossible to come back from the dead.

10. Bob is a simpleton from the country who had an affair during his first marriage. His views on genetically modified organisms are obviously wrong.

11. Many believe that the death penalty is a form of murder. However they are wrong. Killing a human being is called murder, but because one has to be inhumane to commit murder, when applying the death penalty, you are not killing a human. Hence, the death penalty does not constitute murder.

12. Since so many people believe in God, he must exist.

13. The quality of the furniture found at 'Brault & Martineault' is much better than that found at "Meuble Moquin". Just look at how fast Brault & Martineault has been expanding. In the last five years, they opened at least three new stores in the Montreal area alone.

14. This exercise was long and tedious and the teacher should realize that we have many other classes to concentrate on, without mentioning all the homework that we have. Hence we should finish class early today.

Chapter 6 exercises

Read the following passages and identify the fallacy.

1. Anaximander is an Ancient Greek philosopher who lived over 2000 years ago. None of his ideas can have any worth. Hence, there is no point in studying them.
2. Aristotle is a great philosopher because his philosophical ideas were really great.
3. If you do not love Plato, you will never truly love philosophy.
4. There are no records of actual written work by Socrates. All we have are Plato's accounts. So Socrates probably never existed to begin with. He is nothing more than a character invented by Plato.
5. My friend's philosophy teacher wares flip-flops to teach and so does mine. I guess all philosophy teachers wear them to teach.
6. "The Scream" by Munch is a better painting than Monet's "Water lilies" as it makes more noise.
7. If you do not take singing lessons when you are young, you will not be a good singer. This means that you will not be able to go on American Idol and become popular. And if you do not become popular, no one will want to date you and you will remain single for the rest of your life. This is why singing lessons are important.
8. Brad Pitt went to the "Pit-Pit" fashion show and said it was the best show he ever saw. Consequently, the show must be really good and a "must see" when it comes to Montreal.
9. The play I just saw was quite morbid and dark. I am not certain I understood everything. Perhaps if they would have more spotlights on the actors it would create a lighter atmosphere.
10. I am a starving artist. I have to sell my art pieces at ridiculously high amounts if I want to make some kind of living.
11. I saw my teacher at church last Sunday. I guess he must go to church every Sunday.
12. It is written in the Bible that it is the word of God. Since God never lies, then the Bible must be the word of God.
13. So many people believe in God, consequently he must exist.

14. If you are not a good person during your life, you will go to hell when you die.
15. God is known to be the first cause. Since the universe cannot exist without a cause, it clearly shows that God exists.
16. Since nobody can explain where the matter and anti-matter that collided to create the Big Bang came from, the Big Bang theory cannot be taken seriously.
17. If the population does not get their H1N1 flu shot, then the virus will spread, hospitals will be overloaded and children who will get contaminated will not be receiving proper care and will die. Do you want to kill an innocent child? So get your H1N1 flu shot!
18. Aquafresh is better toothpaste than Crest. For one thing, Aquafresh has three colours, which indicates triple action.
19. People should boycott eating poultry products. These poor little birds are squeezed in tiny cages where they cannot move and which they do not leave until they die.
20. Dr. Phil is getting old, his looks are nothing to brag about and he is not a model fitness wise. He is in no position to give advice on how to lead a healthy and happy life.
21. Unless you watch TSN, you will not be able to know anything about the Olympics.
22. Nowadays, everything works with Internet. If you do not know how it works, you will not be able to get a good job. If you do not get a good job, you will not have money and you will not be able to keep your date happy. You will end up alone and sad.
23. I have a Mac computer and have never had any problems with it. If you don't want any problems with your computer, you should get a Mac too.
24. Since cell phones exist, there has been an increase in brain cancer rates. However, no one seems to be able to make a clear relationship between the cancer and the cell phones. Since there is no actual proof that cell phones are responsible for the increase in cancer rates, they should be deemed safe.
25. A woman wrote this critical thinking book. Women are best known for their emotional intelligence and not their logic skills. Also, the author has less than 10 years of college teaching experience. For these reasons, the content of the book cannot be good nor help me learn.

Chapter 7

UNDERSTANDING STATISTICS

Many believe that using statistics is a good way to support a conclusion. For many, numbers are objective and more scientific and hence non-disputable. However, this is not always the case, especially when it comes to statistics. There are several ways statistics can be used to mislead you. The following section will give an overview of the most popular ones.

Unreliable Statistics

Consider the following examples:

Example 37

- *10% of Canadians are homosexuals*
- *35% of teenagers have smoked pot at least once by the time they are 18*
- *5% of women have been battered at least once by their partner* [5]

As convincing as these may be, you should first ask yourself: **"how were these numbers obtained?"** Do you think that everyone who participated in the study was truthful? Would you admit to being gay, smoking pot, being battered…?

[5] These are all fictitious statistics. They only serve to help explain the principle at hand.

Sometimes, it is hard to know how accurate the information is because:

- People are not willing to provide truthful information (such as being gay or using drugs)
- People do not report the events (such as being battered or being raped)
- The event is non-observable (although some homosexuals are more flamboyant than others, you can never be certain unless they provide the information)

If it is unlikely that a precise measurement would be possible, then the statistics only become mere estimates and do not provide strong evidence in an argument. This is why when you come across statistics, you should always ask yourself: "How were these stats gathered? What do they mean exactly?"

Confusing Averages

Consider the following situation:

Example 38

Company X produces the following amounts of air pollution per month:

Jan	*0.50 ppm*
Feb	*0.50 ppm*
March	*0.50 ppm*
April	*0.70 ppm*
May	*0.25 ppm*
June	*0.25 ppm*
July	*0.25 ppm*
Aug.	*0.25 ppm*
Sep.	*0.70 ppm*
Oct.	*0.50 ppm*
Nov.	*7.00 ppm*
Dec.	*0.50 ppm*

The mean of these numbers is: 0.99 ppm
The median of these numbers is: 0.50 ppm
The mode of these numbers is: 0.50 ppm

Now let's say that the safe amount of air pollution is below one ppm on average throughout the year. When you come across "average" values, you should always consider what these numbers mean. In truth, throughout the year, the company in the above example is below one ppm except for the month of November, when the level is nine times what it should be. Does this mean that people who live near the company should not go outside during this month as the air becomes heavily polluted? If you had children and lived close to this company, would you be satisfied to know that on average in a year, its air pollution is below the suggested safe level? Knowing that

November is nine times above safe levels, I would assume and hope that your answer is no.
Every time you see the word 'average', you should remember that there will be some values below and some values above the average. You should always question whether this is relevant or not to the claim being made.

Proving one thing, concluding another

A salesperson from a particular electronics store claims that a particular mp3 player was a big success because only 10 out of 500 buyers who bought the mp3 actually complained to the store about it. The sales person now claims that 98% of its customers are pleased by this particular mp3 and that it is a great buy!

But you should ask yourself: "Does the fact that someone does not come back to the store to complain mean that they are satisfied?" Some people cannot be bothered to go back and complain or ask for a refund.

A better way to assess whether customers are actually satisfied with the product would have been to send a random survey to the 500 people who bought the mp3 and ask them if they were satisfied.

You should always pay close attention to the wording of the statistics and the conclusion that is being drawn from it. You should also ask yourself how you would go about proving such a conclusion and whether the stats actually serve this purpose.

Here is another example:

Example 39

"After surveying a class of fifth graders from a grade school in Westmount Montreal, it was found that half the students in the class had tried smoking pot at least once. Of the 24 students who filled out the survey, 50% of them said that they knew at least one person in their class who had smoked pot."[6]

When you read this quickly, it seems convincing. However, the fact that 12 students in a class know at least one person who smoked pot does not mean that they are referring to 12 different students. They could all know the same student and hence only one student in the class actually used pot. To say that half of the students had tried smoking pot at least once is a gross misinterpretation of the stats that were originally gathered.

Deceiving by Omitting Information

Consider the following statement:

Example 40

"Bob must be a great philosophy teacher as his student dropout rate was 50% less than other teachers in his school last semester."

---

[6] The information in this example is fictitious and only serves to help explain the principle at hand.

Claiming that the number of student drop outs in a class is 50% less only has meaning if you know how many students are dropping out of other classes. For example, it is quite flattering if in other classes, 20 students dropped out and Bob only had 10. However, it becomes quite meaningless if other classes had two and Bob had one—especially if there are 100 students in the class and there are only two teachers.

Year of the sample

It is important to know the year that the sampling took place and ensure that the information is still relevant. Having a source claiming that "70% of Southern Americans own slaves" is not surprising if it is from 1850. However, if it is from 2002, then it certainly becomes more shocking. The year of sample is even more important in fields that are changing at a very rapid rate, such as technologies.

Size of Sample

This is closely linked with the "generalization" fallacy. It is important to ensure that the size of the sample used to create the statistics was adequate. For example, if I say that a survey was given to 10 students at Champlain College and 80% of them said that the Humanities class was fun, it would not have much meaning because the sample group is too small. However, if all Champlain College students were surveyed, then one could assume that Humanities classes at Champlain College are fun.

Biased sample

As the label suggests, this incorrect use of statistics happens when the sample group that was used to gather the statistics was a biased group.

Example 41

"A survey was given to Westmount children asking them what their extracurricular activities were. 67% answered that they took private music lessons on a weekly basis. From this, one can see that Quebec children are musically inclined."[7]

The problem in this example is that Westmount is considered one of Montreal's wealthiest neighborhoods. Hence, the number of children who live in that neighborhood who can afford and who actually take music lessons, is probably not reflective of what other children in Quebec are experiencing. To have a meaningful sample group, you would need to have children from every part of Quebec answering the survey.

Research methods

When provided with a scientific research study, many have a tendency not to question the results of the conclusion as they automatically assume that because it is scientific and conducted by professionals in the field, the results must be reliable. However, scientific research does not mean that it is flawless. There are many factors that could influence a research study and you should keep these in mind as you interpret the results.

For starters, research is done by human beings who could have biased interests in the results. This is commonly seen in the pharmaceutical industry. For example, the pharmaceutical company will provide the grant so that the researcher can look into the side effects of a certain drug. Although the researcher

[7] The information in this example is fictitious and only serves to help explain the principle at hand.

will not falsify results, he could interpret them in a way that is more advantageous to the company.

Another aspect to keep in mind is the research method used. Do the laboratory conditions truly reflect the real world? For example, if a product was shown to have a particular effect on rats, is it reasonable to expect that it will have the same effect on humans? When you read the description of the research project, do you think that it was conducted appropriately? Is there something that was done that could have had an impact on the results (the way the questions were asked, a risk of contaminating the sample…).

When you encounter a statistical figure, you should always ask yourself: "How did they come up with this number?", "Was the procedure used appropriate?" and "Could the results be interpreted differently?" When in doubt, you should try to find other studies that support the findings.

All of what is said above does not mean that the scientific method has no merit. Actually, it is one of our best sources of evidence. This is mainly due to the fact that the scientific method implies that the researchers will provide the materials and methods used to conduct the experiment so that anyone who wishes to reproduce the experiment can do so. This means that anyone can recreate the conditions of testing and verify that the results are the same.

ACTIVITY 7

Read the following passages and determine what is wrong with the statistics presented in them.

a) 2% of Canadians like to urinate in public showers.

b) 200 men living near Beaudry metro in Montreal were asked to fill out a questionnaire on their sexuality. 175 of them answered that they are homosexuals. This shows that 87.5% of men in Montreal are homosexuals.

c) The average amount of lead found in deer in the Laurentians is below the suggested safety zone proposed by Health Canada. Hence all deer caught in the Laurentians are safe to eat (Albert, 2005, p.47).

d) Five Montreal women were asked what they thought about war. Four of them answered that they were against it. Hence, 80% of women in Montreal are against war.

e) Fizz aspirin works 50% faster (Headache, 2005, p.69).

f) 1000 Montreal women were asked what they thought about war. 700 of them answered that they were against it. Hence, 70% of women in Montreal are against war (Foggy, 1914, p.9).

g) In September 2004, a college teacher asked his students "Would you be content to only watch Hollywood movies if you knew that the government money that was spent in supporting the Canadian movies industry would be used in the health sector instead?" 68% of the students answered "yes". The teacher concluded that only 32% of his students enjoy Canadian movies (Albert, 2005, p.47).

Chapter 7 exercises

Read the following passages and determine what is wrong with the statistics presented in them.

1. All of Plato's students were asked if they liked philosophy. 100% of them answered yes. This clearly shows that all students like philosophy.
2. 100% of the essays I read say that Socrates was an ugly man. This shows that he was an ugly man.
3. 10 students were asked if they like their "philosophy and the ancient world" class. 8 of them answered yes. This means that 80% of students like philosophy and the ancient world.
4. In the year 350 BCE, 57% of the people living in Greece said they knew at least one famous philosopher. Considering the size of the population, that makes a lot of philosophers!
5. 1% of sophists have resorted to prostitution to make ends meet.
6. In 1989, nobody thought that web design was an art form.
7. I was told that the average price of a painting in that art gallery is 700$. Since I know that she likes that gallery and that I wanted to offer her a graduation gift of around 700$, I sent my niece to buy a painting of her choice there.
8. A survey was given to over a 1000 students of various high schools asking them what kind of music they like. The results show that 14% of high school boys like classical music.
9. I was told that Bilodeau's sculptures are 40% bigger. I guess I will not have room in my house for them.
10. The most expensive piece of art ever sold in a public auction is Picasso's "Garçon à la pipe". It went for 104 200 000$. (Art World, 2004)
11. A study was conducted amongst security guards from several prisons in Crimeland. 96% of them said that the most violent criminal they knew was an atheist. This clearly shows that the religious are less likely to be violent.
12. We wanted to know how many people in Pretend Town actually went to church. To ensure that many people would answer, we gave out the survey in the town church, right after the Sunday morning sermon. The results showed that 94% of the citizens of Pretend Town attend church on a regular basis.

13. 10 teenagers were asked if it was important for them to be married before they had sex. 1 of them answered yes and the rest of them answered no. This clearly shows that only 10% of teenagers want to wait to be married before they have sex.
14. The average salary in Pretend Town is 33 000$ a year. The Scientology church believes that their disciples should give 10% of their salary, so they require all followers of Pretend Town to give 3 300$ annually.
15. There are 2000 active members in the Raëlian movement (Ufo, 1978, p.69)
16. A study was conducted on the 10 most popular cell phones on the market and the radiation levels they emit. On average, the radiation levels were below the maximum safety level.
17. Expecto cough syrup works 20% faster.
18. 98% of pharmaceutical company owners claim that the H1N1 flu shot must be given to everyone.
19. 5 gynecologists were asked what they thought of practicing voluntary c-sections. 3 of them answered that they were against such a practice. Hence, 60% of gynecologists are against it.
20. 100 teachers from a school district were asked if they knew a teacher who underwent plastic surgery. One out of three of them answered yes. Consequently, 33% of teachers in that district have undergone plastic surgery.
21. 8% of teens have Internet gambling problems.
22. My ten best friends each have at least 10 friends on Facebook. This means that through my friends on Facebook, I can make at least 100 more friends.
23. Only 20% of Canadian families currently own a computer. (Fake, 1993)
24. 500 men were asked if they read Elle magazine. Only 40 of them answered yes. This means that only 8% of the population reads Elle magazine.
25. 15 students were asked if they usually complete every exercise in their book. Three of them answered "yes, up until the very last one!" We can infer that only 20% of students completed all exercises in this book.

Chapter 

ANALYZING A THESIS ESSAY

You have now seen all elements needed to properly analyze a thesis essay. All that is left to do is to bring them together, learn a few helpful tricks and of course, practice. Read the following essay and try to:

1. Find the premises and write the argument in standardized form.
2. Decide whether you should use inductive or deductive logic.
3. If the argument is deductive, say whether it is sound or not and explain why.
4. If the argument is inductive, say whether it is weak or strong.

Be sure to give a detailed analysis of each premise while explaining your answer.

The Truth about Newspaper Recycling

Many believe that newspaper recycling has a number of environmental benefits. The production of recycled paper requires less water and energy than the production of virgin fiber for example. It is also a good way to eliminate the amount of waste going into landfill sites. In light of these benefits, recycling newspaper is not the environmental solution bragged about. This essay will show that newspaper recycling does not offer a solution to our environmental problems as it cannot be done indefinitely, it does not necessarily save trees and it produces harmful chemical waste in our environment.

Paper cannot be recycled indefinitely. After five to eight trips to the mill, the fibers become too short to be useful. Recycled fibers may be too weak to be used in some types of paper unless they are reinforced with virgin pulp. This means that to ensure a certain quality of paper, virgin fibers are always added and thus needed. It is unrealistic to think that we could only use recycled paper.

Also, recycled paper cannot be used everywhere. Some high-quality papers used for photocopying or for printing posters, for example, will still have to be made from virgin pulp. It is estimated that high-quality papers represent at least 43% of the world's paper production.

Most interesting, is the fact that recycling will not necessarily save the trees. About half the wood used in papermaking comes from wood chips and other waste left over by the lumber industry. Wood chips cannot be left in the environment as it prevents vegetation from growing. If it is not used for paper production, then it will be wasted. In this sense, paper production is good for the environment and uses material that would otherwise be wasted.

Furthermore, recycling produces its own waste. The ink that is removed from the paper forms a 'sludge' that has to be disposed of somehow. One ton of old newspapers can produce up to 200 kilograms of the stuff. Some claim the sludge is non-toxic; it has even been used as fertilizer. However, new research shows that it is not safe and that this 'sludge' takes more time to exit the environment than paper would have taken to decompose. Indeed, Dr. Richard conducted a study in which he compared the decomposition rate of virgin paper with that of sludge. According to his research, the sludge can take up to 60 years to be eliminated from the environment whereas the paper will be fully decomposed within less than 10 years. This does not take into account the fact that the sludge pollutes the water.

Hence, when one considers that paper production is actually good for the environment, that paper decomposes faster than the chemical residues of recycling and that recycled paper cannot be used everywhere, it is clear that the recycling of newspaper does not offer a solution to our environmental problems. In fact, one should question whether it does not worsen the problem.

*This essay was written by Denise Albert so that students could practice their critical thinking skills. It does not reflect her views.

If you follow this list, you should have no trouble finding the argument and analyzing it properly.

1. **Read the essay**
   a. Reading the entire essay at least once will give you an overall picture of what is being discussed.
2. **Find the conclusion of the argument**
   If you do not know what the conclusion of the argument is, it is very hard to find the premises. This is why you should always identify the conclusion first.
   a. **Read the introduction and find the thesis statement**. In a well-written essay, the author will state the conclusion of the argument in the introduction. This is what we call a thesis statement. As you read the introduction, you should ask yourself: "What is the author trying to show?" or "What will be the point of this essay?"
   b. **Read the conclusion and ensure that you found the correct thesis**. In a well-written essay, the

thesis will be repeated in the conclusion of the essay. Hence, you should always skip directly to the conclusion and ensure that the thesis statement you found in the introduction is the same one that appears in the conclusion. If both are the same, then you have found the conclusion of the argument being presented in the essay.

3. **Find the premises**
   a. **In a well-written essay, one paragraph means one premise**. Since there should never be any premises in the introduction or the conclusion of an essay, if your essay has six paragraphs (as the above example does), you can assume that there will be four premises.
   b. **Find the topic sentence**. In a well-written essay, each paragraph will start with a topic sentence. Since the rest of the paragraph is supposed to support and explain the topic sentence, the topic sentence should be a premise in the argument of the essay. Usually, the topic sentence of an essay is the first sentence of the paragraph. However, it could be the case that it is the last sentence. This will depend on the writing style of the author. Moreover, a topic sentence should NEVER be in the middle of a paragraph.
4. **Write the argument in standardized form**
   a. Now that you have all your premises and your conclusion, this should be quite simple.
5. **Determine whether the argument is valid**
   a. Determining the validity of the argument will get you thinking about the connection between the premises and the conclusion and this will help you determine whether the argument is deductive or inductive. If you are still confused, keep in mind that most arguments that are presented in essays are inductive.
      b. Assumptions. You should also question whether any assumptions are being made and whether these assumptions should have been explained. For example:

i. A cotton coat will only keep you warm in temperatures above 5ºC
ii. A cotton coat is not waterproof
iii. A cotton coat will not repel snow
iv. Therefore, a cotton coat would not be adequate for Canadian winters

In this particular example, there is an assumption being made that Canadian winters are colder than 5ºC and that there is snow.

Assumption 1: Canadian Winters are wet, snowy and colder than 5ºC

i. A cotton coat will only keep you warm in temperatures above 5ºC
ii. A cotton coat is not water proof
iii. A cotton coat will not repel snow
iv. Therefore, a cotton coat would not be adequate for Canadian winters

This assumption does not need to be clearly stated as it is common knowledge. Anyone who lives in Canada would make sense of the argument without this information being clearly stated. On the other hand, consider the following example:

i. Killing a human being is called murder
ii. Murder is wrong
iii. Abortion is the killing of a fetus
iv. Therefore abortion is wrong

In this particular example, assumptions are being made: One, is that the fetus is a human being and two, is that abortion is murder. The argument could be rewritten in the following form:

i. Killing a human being is called murder
ii. Murder is wrong
iii. Abortion is the killing of a fetus

Assumption 1: a fetus is a human being
Assumption 2: abortion is murder

iv. Therefore abortion is wrong

The idea that the fetus is a human being is highly controversial. In fact it is the essence of the whole debate. This needs to be stated and justified. It cannot merely be assumed. If the first assumption was properly explained and justified, then the second assumption becomes acceptable.

When assessing the validity of an argument, you should consider whether any assumptions need to be identified and if these assumptions are acceptable or not. Since some premises are supported with sub-arguments, you should also keep assumptions in mind as you are assessing the truth of premises.

6. **Establish the truth of each premise**
   a. **You must ensure that each premise is well supported and not merely an opinion**. To do this, you must read the entire paragraph that pertains to the premise and question whether the paragraph justifies the truth of the premise. If it is an acceptable premise, then you should clearly state why by using the course terminology learned thus far (for example, it is supported by a figure of authority). If the premise is not acceptable, you also need to clearly state why (for example, there is a “red herring fallacy”). If you find that the paragraph does not support the premise, then the premise is not acceptable and it becomes mere opinion and this will weaken the argument.
   b. **To maximize your success in this task, you should use the list of acceptable premises, non-acceptable premises, fallacies, deceiving statistics and assumptions**. Each time you read a paragraph, go through your lists one item at a time and question whether it applies to the paragraph. If you find something that applies, you

should keep searching. The more you have to say about a premise, the better. Although this might seem long and tedious at first, as you practice, eventually, you will not need your lists anymore as you will have developed your critical thinking skills.

7. **Determine the quality of the argument**
   a. If using deductive logic, then the overall analysis is easier. Depending on the validity and the truth of the premises, you can simply conclude that the argument is sound or not sound. There is no need to do the next step.
   b. If using inductive logic (which is what you will mostly be using in this class), more will need to be discussed. An inductive argument can be weak or strong and anything in between. Here is a list of adjectives that could be used to describe an argument:
      i. Very weak
      ii. Weak
      iii. Not convincing
      iv. Convincing
      v. Strong
      vi. Very strong
      vii. Interesting
      viii. Thought provoking
      ix. Lacking
      x. ...

8. **Give your overall comments on the argument**
   a. Simply stating that the argument is weak or strong is not enough. You must explain your statement. For example, if the argument has four very good premises and one weak premise, will you say that the whole argument is weak? Perhaps you will say that the argument is convincing but that it could be made stronger by changing the weak premise.

ACTIVITY 8

Read the following essay and try to:

1. **Find the premises and write the argument in standardized form.**
2. **Decide whether you should use inductive or deductive logic.**
3. **If the argument is deductive, say whether it is sound or not and explain why.**
4. **If the argument is inductive, say whether it is weak or strong.**

Be sure to give a detailed analysis of each premise while explaining your answer

The Truth about ASR Tires

Since the arrival of All Season Radial tires in the 1970s, preparing for winter in Quebec has brought on a new dilemma: Are snow tires necessary? Thinking of the added costs and hassle of snow tires, more and more Quebeckers are turning to All Season Radial tires. This paper will show that snow tires continue to be the very best way of assuring a safe vehicle during Quebec's winter months.

According to Elaine Pfrimmer, ASR tires are not as safe and lead to accidents. As she was driving home one winter, her car began to slide: "I'm trying so hard to pump the brake, gently, and pulling to the left for all I'm worth, and this car is still going to the right," Pfrimmer recalls. "There was just no other option; I was going where this car wanted to go." (CBC Marketplace, 1998, ¶ 3) In the end, she was lucky and only ran into a telephone pole and no one was seriously hurt. The tires on her car that night were All Season Radials, not snow tires. Pfrimmer wrongly thought that her ASR tires would carry her safely through the winter (CBC Marketplace, 1998, ¶ 3). This is one of many stories that could be given as an example to show that ASR tires are not safe for winter conditions.

ASR tires are not designed to perform adequately in Quebec cold winter weather. Between -8°C and -15°C, the rubber of ASR hardens and loses its grip on the road (Société d'Assurance Automobile du Québec, 2004). "The reality is the chemical compounds of the rubber that we need in Canada have to be pliable in cold temperatures. All Season Radials don't have the ability to stay pliable when the temperature drops" (CBC News Online, 2004, ¶ 6). On the other hand, snow tires have a tread that bites more in the snow. "Also, winter tires have compounds that keep rubber more pliable for better grip as it gets colder" (Jensen, 2004, ¶ 9).

Furthermore, winter tires provide better control than ASR ones. A braking test was done and it was shown that cars with winter tires do not skid as much as ASR ones. It was actually shown that ASR tires will skid 12% further than winter tires (CBC Marketplace-Putting tires to the test, 1998, ¶ 8). Additionally, a study conducted by the Quebec Ministry of Transport showed that winter tires can improve collision avoidance by about 38% (CBC News Online, 2004, ¶ 11).

This essay has shown that ASR tires are not safe enough for Quebec Winter conditions, that winter tires are better designed for cold weather and that they provide better control. Consequently, it is evident that snow tires are the best option for Quebec drivers. ASR tires are not the right choice for Quebec winters. If you are at all concerned about safe driving this winter, you will choose to install a good set of snow tires and save your ASR ones for warmer and better driving conditions.

References:

CBC Marketplace (1998, November 3). *Getting a grip: Are your all-season tires really equipped?* Retrieved May 3, 2005 from http://www.cbc.ca/consumers/ market/files/cars/tires/

CBC Marketplace (1998 , November 3). *Putting tires to the test.* Retrieved May 3, 2005 from http://www.cbc.ca/consumers/market /files/cars/tires/tiretests.html

CBC News Online (2004, December 8). *Winter Tires: Making a comeback.* Retrieved May 3, 2005 from http://www.cbc.ca/news/background/consumertips/ wintertires.html

Etkin, David (No date) The Social and Economic Impact of Hydrometeorological Hazards and Disasters: a Preliminary Inventory. *Coping with Natural Hazards in Canada: Scientific, Government and Insurance Industry Perspectives; part 2: natural hazards in Canada* Retreived May 3, 2005 from http://www.utoronto.ca/env/nh/pt2ch4-4.htm

Jensen, Cheryl (2004, December 5). *Getting a grip on snow with the right tires*. Retrieved May 3, 2005 from http://www.stangbangers.com/Snow_Tires.htm

Radio Canada (2004, January 30). *Aujourd'hui*. Retreived May 3, 2005 from http://radio-canada.ca/actualite/placepublique/messages.asp?clip=862

SAAQ (2004, 1e trimestre) Avez-vous les bons pneus pour déjouer l'hiver? *Info SAAQ Bulletin no 4.* Retrieved May 3, 2005 from http://www.saaq.gouv.qc.ca/ publications/prevention /infosaaq/infosaaq_04f.pdf

*This essay was written by Denise Albert so that students could practice their critical thinking skills. It does not reflect her views.

Chapter 8 exercises

Read the following essays[8] and try to:

1. **Find the premises and write the argument in standardized form.**
2. **Decide whether you should use inductive or deductive logic.**
3. **If the argument is deductive, say whether it is sound or not and explain why.**
4. **If the argument is inductive, say whether it is weak or strong.**

Be sure to give a detailed analysis of each premise while explaining your answer

The contemporary relevance of Greek mythology

Each culture seems to have a particular way of explaining the origin of the world, the meaning of life and what is good and evil. In ancient Greece, people looked to Greek mythology for their answers. Even though this system of belief is more than 2000 years old, this essay will show that it still has contemporary significance and relevance. Whether it be the genesis or the creation of the various gods, there are several elements that reflect present day life.

According to Greek mythology, the first god to come into being was Chaos. As the story goes, first there was nothing, and out of this nothingness, a gap was created: Chaos. Within this void called Chaos emerged Gaia, known as mother earth, Eros (love), Tartarus (underworld) and Erebus (darkness). This is quite similar to the Big Bang theory: First there was nothing, and then a big

[8] All essays in this section were written by Denise Albert so that students could practice their critical thinking skills. They do not reflect her views.

explosion caused chaos within the universe. From this chaotic unorganized expansion of matter, after billion of years, the earth was created. Both the scientific and the mythological account refer to chaos and say that the earth came from that chaos. Clearly, Greek mythology offers similarities with the scientific version of the creation of the universe.

The story goes on to tell that Gaia (mother earth) gives birth asexually to Uranus (the sky), who then fertilizes her and gives rise to the Titans, the Cyclopes (one eyed giants) and Hecatonchires (giants each possessing 100 hands and fifty heads). This is a clear example of what happens if a mother and son create offsprings together: their children run the risk of having some kind of genetic abnormality and being as ugly as the Cyclopes and Hecatonchires. This passage also reflects the existence of monsters in our society. In myth and in present day, consanguinity can lead to genetic malformations.

Eventually, Cronus (a male Titan -the youngest of Gaia's children) will castrate his father Uranus; then will become the ruler of Gods with his sister Rhea and they will give birth to the Olympians. This is a clear example of how every son wants to overpower his father. A perfect example of this is Oedipus, who killed his father Laius, to couple with his mother Jocasta, queen of Thebes. (wikipedia) As shown, Greek mythology accounts for Freud's Oedipus complex.

In conclusion, considering that Greek mythology offers similarities with the scientific version of the creation of the universe, that its incestuous relationships lead to genetic malformations and that Freud's Oedipus complex is clearly represented, one can definitely say that Greek mythology has contemporary significance and relevance. This leads one to wonder what inspired the creation of the myths to begin with. Could it really be that within the last 3000 years, humanity has not changed that much?

Pablo Picasso's value

Born in 1881, Pablo Picasso is one of the greatest figures of 20th-century modern art (Buchholz, Bühler, Hille, Kaeppele and Stotland, 2007, p.428). However, many do not understand what is so special about his art and why it is considered art to begin with. This essay will show that Picasso's art has great value because he was famous, he created cubism and because he sold the most expensive art piece ever.

To begin with, Picasso's art is art of great value because he was famous. Picasso was famous because he was renowned for his artwork. According to most, his art is priceless. There is even an "I love Picasso far too much" group on Facebook where 24 group members write how much they admire Picasso.

Also, Picasso created what is known today as cubism. "Les Demoiselles d'Avignon" depicts human figures from different viewpoints. This became one of the characteristic features of cubism. The idea was to depict three-dimensional objects into a two-dimensional plane. It is important to note that Picasso was not alone in the creation of cubism. Although he is not as famous and his artwork is not worth as much, Georges Braque also shares the honour of creating cubism.

Finally, the most expensive art piece ever sold in an auction is a Picasso. Indeed, on May 2004, "Garçon à la pipe" sold for 104.2 million US$ at Sotheby. This established a new price record. (Wikipedia) This painting was done in 1905 when Picasso was 24 years old during his "Rose Period".(Wikipedia)

Thus, because Picasso was famous, created cubism and sold the most expensive art piece ever, it is clear that his art is art and that it has great value. Perhaps when you look at one of his paintings you may think that a five year old could do the same. But the point is that Picasso wanted his paintings to look that way; he wanted to be different and push the art movement further.

Bibliography

Buchholz E., Bühler G., Hille K., Kaeppele S.& Stotland, I. (2007). *ART a world history*, New York; Abrams

The hijab: Confusing religion and culture

The Quebec's advisory council on the status of women recommended that women in public service jobs who interact with the public should be prohibited from wearing any obvious religious signs. As a result, opposition parties are pressuring the liberal government to define its position on the delicate issue of Muslim women who wear the hijab in public sector positions. This whole debate rests on the notion that the hijab is a “religious sign”. However, this notion is false. As this essay will show, the hijab is not a religious sign or symbol. The hijab is nothing more than a fashion statement derived from culture and not religion.

To begin with, hijab is an Arabic word that means: curtain or cover. When analyzing the root of the word, it means to cover, to veil or shelter. The word used in the Qur'an to refer to a veil or headscarf is khimar, not hijab. This clearly shows that there is no religious connotation to the word hijab.

In fact, there is nothing in the Qur'an that says that women must wear the hijab. According to a posting on Wikipedia, the Qur'an instructs the male believers to talk to wives of Muhammad behind a hijab (which is meant to be understood as a curtain that divides or provides privacy). Furthermore, this hijab was the responsibility of the men and not the wives of Muhammad. (Wikipedia, hijab, ¶3). What the Qur'an does instruct is to dress in a modest way. Actually, there are several Muslims who believe that the commandment to modesty must be obeyed in relation to the society they live in. What is considered modest in one society may not be considered so in another. In this sense, it is clear that the hijab is a matter of culture and not religion.

If the commandment to modesty depends on the society one lives in, then the hijab can be nothing more than a fashion statement. In fact, there are several websites and books that discuss the various ways the hijab should be worn. Websites such as "We love our hijabs" discuss how you can attend hijab fashion shows, like BCBG Max Azria's Fall 2010 ready to wear collection. It also states that fashion designer Christian Lacroix offers such a thing as designer hijabs. More impressively, it has a links to ideeli.com, which is an "invitation-only" shopping website that offers limited time sales events on designer brands at discount prices. I have never heard or seen any religious symbol that was also fashion-wear at the same time. Fashion is related to culture and not religion.

After everything is said and done, it is clear that the hijab is not a religious symbol. As it has been shown, the Arabic word has no religious connotation; there is nothing in the Qur'an that instructs women to wear it because in the end, it is nothing more than a piece of clothing subject to fashion, like any other piece of clothing. When you think about it, if the hijab was meant to be a religious symbol, then wouldn't all Muslim women wear it?

The truth about cell phones

When cell phones were introduced over a decade ago, only the rich could actually afford to buy them. Today, however, it is estimated that 83% of the Quebec population owns a cell phone (Statistic Canada, 2007, p773). Because of its growing popularity, there is growing concern about safety, environmental and health issues. Following a discussion on all the new research that has been done on cell phones, it will become quite evident to the reader that cell phones should not be manufactured or sold to teenagers.

First off, according to a study done by the Land Line research institute, cell phones increase your chances of getting a brain tumor by 12% (Phoneb, 2007, p. 77). Indeed a correlation was found between cell phone use and the occurrence of brain tumors. Dr. George Carlo who was chairman of Wireless Technology Research reported that there is reason to be alarmed if using cell phones: "According to recent research, using a cell phone on a regular basis increases your chances of getting a brain tumor" (Carlo, 2007, p. 33).

Secondly, there is strong evidence that cell phones lead to the premature loss of hearing in adults. In fact, Tom Hanks always used his right hand and right ear when talking on a cell phone and now, at age 49, he must wear a hearing aid (Hanks, 2006, par. 2). He is one of many of his generation that now has to wear a hearing aid. In fact, a study conducted in Quebec shows that in 1980, only 15% of people between the ages of 50 and 65 had to wear hearing aids. However, today, more than 36% of adults in the same age range are wearing hearing aids (Statistic Canada, 2007, par. 4). This is clear evidence that cell phones are causing premature hearing loss.

Furthermore, cell phones are bad for the environment. Cell phones have become somewhat of a fashion accessory. There are new models with new features, colours and designs coming out on the market every year. This encourages people to change their cell phones on a yearly basis. But what is done with the old ones? Unfortunately, most throw it away, which means more stuff in our landfills. This increased pollution is not helping the global warming situation that we are faced with. If anything, it is accelerating the process and leading us to increased natural disasters and human death tolls. This does not take into account the Electrical Magnetic Field, waves and radiations that cell phones produce in the environment. It was shown that Odif cell phones produce all three at dangerously high levels.

Therefore, although cell phones seem to be harmless and fun, quite the contrary is true. They can cause tumors and premature hearing loss as well as pollute the environment needlessly. From this, it is quite clear that cell phones should not be manufactured or sold to teenagers. In fact, one should question whether they should be sold to anyone.

Bibliography

Carlo, George (2007) What cell phones do to our brains. *Journal of Wireless Technology*. Vol.5 (6) pp. 34-39

Hanks, Tom (2006) an Interview with Tom Hanks. Retrieved Sept. 27th, 2007 from http://www.oprah.com

Phoneb, Jill. (2007). Cell phones and brain tumors. *Journal of technology*. Vol 3 (2) pp. 58-80

Statistic Canada (2007).Retrieved on Sept. 27th, 2007 from: http://www.statcan.ca/Daily/English/070628.htm

Vaccination is the disease, not the cure

In 1796, Edward Jenner created the first vaccine by infecting a patient with cowpox in an attempt to create immunization against small pox. More than 200 years later, vaccination has become a prerequisite for school admission in several states in the US. (Wikipedia) However, since the 1980s, there has been growing concern on the safety and efficiency of vaccination. It has become quite clear that there is no evidence that it eliminated childhood diseases, it comes with significant risks and its immunization is only short lived. Parents who love their children should not get them vaccinated.

There is no scientific evidence that mass inoculations can be credited with eliminating childhood diseases. Vaccination has never actually been clinically proven to be effective in preventing disease. No researcher has directly exposed test subjects to disease (for ethical reasons) (Healing Daily, 2002, ¶ 8). According to Dr. Robert Mendelsohn, "While it is true that some once common childhood diseases have diminished or disappeared since inoculations were introduced, no one really knows why" (1984, ¶ 5). For example, In 1958 there were about 800,000 cases of measles in the United States, but by 1965, before the first measles shot, the death rate had declined to only 0.03 deaths per 100,000 (Mendesohn, 1984, ¶ 23).

There are significant risks associated with immunization. There is growing suspicion that immunization against relatively harmless childhood diseases may be responsible for the dramatic increase in auto-immune diseases since mass inoculations were introduced. For example, California's autism rate has mushroomed 1000% over the past 20 years, with dramatic increases following the introduction of the MMR vaccine in the early 80's (Healing Daily, 2002, ¶23). More interestingly, the FDA estimates that as few as 1% of serious adverse reactions to vaccines are ever reported (Healing Daily, 2002, ¶12).

Immunization from vaccination is only short lived. A large proportion of children show no evidence of immunity in blood tests given only four or five years after rubella vaccination (Mendelsohn, 1984, ¶ 31). According to Mendelsohn, "the significance of this is both obvious and frightening. Rubella is a non threatening disease in childhood, and it confers natural immunity to those who contract it so they will not get it again as adults [...] Today, because of immunization, the vast majority of women never acquire natural immunity. If their vaccine-induced immunity wears off, they may contract rubella while they are pregnant, with resulting damage to their unborn children."(1984, ¶32-33)

Pharmaceutical companies are making a fortune with the mandatory vaccination programs. However, there is no evidence that mass vaccination is responsible for the elimination of childhood diseases. Furthermore, there are significant risks associated with vaccination while its immunization is only short lived. When all is considered, parents who love their children should not get them vaccinated. In fact, perhaps it is time we question whether we have traded mumps and measles for cancer and leukemia.

Bibliography

Healing Daily, (2002). Vaccines: know the risk. Healing Daily. Retrieved March 14th 2010 from http://www.healingdaily.com

Mendolsohn, Robert (1984). The Medical Time Boomb of Immunization Against Disease. Whale Retrieved from http://www.whale.to/vaccines/mendelsohn.html

Chapter 9

WRITING A THESIS ESSAY

Equally important to the task of being capable of analyzing an argument found in an essay is the ability to create, express and defend your own ideas. The following section will try to give you various tips to help you write a clear, coherent and flowing essay.

Finding a Topic

The first element that is needed when writing an essay is a GOOD topic. The narrower your topic will be the easier it will be for you to write a clear and coherent essay. Consider, for example, the two topics below:

a) Ritalin
b) The use of Ritalin in grade school children in North America

Because the second topic is more focused in terms of age group and location, the writer will necessarily be more focused in the information provided. Also, having a narrow topic will ensure that your argument will be stronger as it will be harder to find counter examples. For instance, one could not use information about Ritalin used in Europe or Asia or used in teenagers to find counter examples to the premises as it is outside the scope of the topic.

When thinking about your topic, keep the five 'W's in mind:

Who
Where
When
Why
What

The 'What' will be your general topic and you should add at least two other 'W's. In the above example we had:

What: Ritalin
Who: Grade School Children
Where: In North America

Another example would be:

What: Educational system
Where: Quebec
When: Between 1945 and 1955

Doing Research

Doing a 'Google search' or using any other similar search engine to find information on your topic is fine to get you started and to give you ideas or general information. However, most web links provided by such searches are NOT credible sources. Before using any information found, you should ensure that the source is credible ('.edu' or '.gov' websites for example), that the year of publication is relevant, that there is an author to the information (whether an individual or organization) and that this author is a reliable figure of authority in the subject matter. A much better way to find information that is certain to be credible is to use the academic search engines provided by your school library (Ebscohost is a good example). If you do not know what this is or how to use it, you should not be shy to go see your librarian for help.

If your teacher did not specify the amount of sources needed, as a general rule, you should have one source per essay content page that you must write (the introduction and conclusion space should not be counted here). Hence, for a five-page essay, you should have about four sources and if you are writing a 10-page essay, you should have about eight sources.

As you read your sources, you should highlight all passages that you think could be relevant. You should also put notes in the margins—just a word or two to trigger your memory as to what that information pertains to. Doing this will save you a lot of time. You must remember that you will be reading several sources of several pages each. You need a system to remember where what information is, without having to re-read the whole article again. Taking notes in the margin is a great way to achieve this.

Example 42

Good Internet Sources	However, most web links provided by such searches are NOT credible sources. Before using any information found, you should ensure that the source is credible ('.edu' or '.gov' websites for example), that the year of publication is relevant and that there is an author to the information (whether an individual or organization). A much better way to find information that is certain to be credible is to use the academic search engines provided by your school library (Ebscohost is a good example). If you do not know what this is or how to use it, you should go see your librarian for help. A librarian is a trained professional in research. Asking for help will not only be extremely formative for you, but it will also save you a lot of time.

If you cannot write on your source, then you will need to take notes on a separate sheet of paper. Before you take notes on a source, you should always ensure that you write up the bibliographical information on it first and that you keep track of page numbers (or paragraph numbers for websites without page numbers). Again, you should put key words in the margin to trigger your memory as to where which information is.

Example 43

Good Internet Sources	Albert, Denise (2007). *Critical Thinking for College Students*. Montreal: Denise Albert. • A credible internet source should have .edu or .gov. and should have an author (p.60) • Use academic search engines like Ebscohost (p. 60)

Creating a Thesis Statement

A thesis statement is a sentence that expresses the goal of your essay. It is the conclusion of the argument that will be defended. Once you have read various sources on your topic, it should become clear to you what the thesis of your essay will be and you should be able to express it clearly within one sentence. For example:

Example 44

"The use of Ritalin in grade school children should not be encouraged as long-term effects of this drug have yet to be studied."

You should notice that when reading the thesis statement, the topic is clearly stated (Ritalin in grade school children) as well as the particular position being defended (that it should not be used) in addition to one of the main reasons that will support the claim (because long-term effects of this drug have yet to be studied). As you can see, from reading this one sentence, it is very clear to the reader what will be discussed in the essay and what the objective of it is. On the other hand, if all that was written was:

"This essay will discuss the use of Ritalin in North American grade school children"

This is not a thesis statement. It is not precise enough. Although it does inform the reader on the topic discussed, it does not mention what the point of the essay will be. A good thesis statement needs to inform the reader on the objective of the essay. It needs to actually spell out what the conclusion will be.

If you are not a very good writer, here are a few different 'fill in the blanks' thesis structures that you can use (although using them will not give you good literary style, at least they will ensure clarity).

A) This essay will show that ____________________ in ____________ is ____________ because ________________________.

B) Seeing as ______________________________ it is clear that (or it will be shown that) ________________.

C) Through ________________________________, it will be shown that ______________________________.

D) Following a discussion and explanation of ____________________________, it will be evident that ______________________.

At the very least, you need to ensure that your thesis statement includes:

- Your topic (with at least two 'W's)
- The position being defended
- A brief account of the main reason that will be given to support your position

You should also keep in mind that it is a statement and not a question. It needs to be clear and explicit (Your essay should not be a mystery essay where the conclusion of the argument is given away within the very last paragraph).

Writing an Essay Outline

Before you actually start writing a draft of your essay, you should always take the time to plan out your essay by writing an outline. In essence, your outline is a standardized version of the argument that will be presented in your essay. There are several ways to structure an outline; this is the one suggested:

Example 45

***Introduction**:*
Thesis statement…………………………………………………

Background information on the topic
(Do you need a paragraph of background information on the topic?)
What
Who
When
Why
Where
…..

***Premise 1**:* ………………………………………………………….

a) *1st reason to accept Premise (fact or information that supports it)*
b) *2nd reason to accept Premise (fact or information that supports it)*
c) ...

***Premise 2**: ………………………………………………………….*
d) *1st reason to accept Premise (fact or information that supports it)*
e) *2nd reason to accept Premise (fact or information that supports it)*
f) ...

***Premise 3**: ……………………………………………………….*
g) *1st reason to accept Premise (fact or information that supports it)*
h) *2nd reason to accept Premise (fact or information that supports it)*
i) ...

***Objection and Reply**: ……………………………………….*
(Ensure that your teacher asked you to add this in your essay)
(Ensure that it is the main objection that can be made)

Conclusion

Writing an Introduction

The purpose of an introduction is to ease the reader into the topic as well as inform on what the thesis will be. Hence, it should always start with a few lines that serve to gently establish what the topic of the essay will be. Considering that the first sentence of your introduction is what will set the tone of your essay, you should always ensure that you spend extra time on it.

Once the topic has been established, you should state your thesis. Following this, you should add a few lines to help better define what your essay will be about. For example, you could discuss the limits or scopes of your topic. You could also discuss the general strategy indented to support your thesis.

Hence, a good introduction is composed of three essential parts:

A) Easing the reader into the topic
B) Stating thesis
C) Defining limits, scope and/or general strategy

Most importantly, you need to ensure that you have proper flow between these different sections

Example 46

Contrary to what many believe, Attention Deficit Hyperactive Disorder (ADHD) is not a new disease. It can actually be traced back as far as 1902 when an English pediatrician, Still, gave the first description of hyperactivity (Ross & Ross, p. 14-15). More than 30 years after, in 1937, Bradley discovered a medication that could help alleviate the symptoms associated with the disorder. Bradley prescribed Benzedrine, an amphetamine, for emotionally disturbed children who were in a residential treatment centre in an effort to rid them of severe headaches by raising their blood pressure. To his surprise, the children underwent a dramatic change characterized by increased interest in schoolwork, better work habits, and a marked reduction in disruptive behavior (Ross & Ross, p. 16). Since then, many other psychotropic drugs for ADHD children have entered the market, the most famous one being methylphenidate, better known under its brand name "Ritalin". However, due to its growing popularity, one should perhaps question whether we should be concerned about giving this drug on a regular basis to children. Using a basically consequentialist approach, this essay will show that although many of the worries surrounding Ritalin consumption in children are ill-founded the long term use of Ritalin in grade school children should be banned since no data is available concerning the long-term side effects of the drug. In order to show this, an explanation of what ADHD is exactly, as well as discussion of what is believed to cause the disorder will be given. This being done, it will be easier to understand why treatment is needed and what options are available to the patients. This background information will eliminate many possible misconceptions and will enable a better understanding of what should be the central ethical debate surrounding the use of Ritalin in children.

A shorter version of the same introduction would be:

Example 47

Contrary to what many believe, Attention Deficit Hyperactive Disorder (ADHD) is not a new disease. It can actually be traced back as far as 1902 when an English pediatrician, Still, gave the first description of hyperactivity (Ross & Ross, p. 14-15). 100 years later, many psychotropic drugs for ADHD children have entered the market, the most famous one being methylphenidate, better known under its brand name "Ritalin". However, due to its growing popularity, one should perhaps question whether we should be concerned about giving this drug on a regular basis to children. Using a basically consequentialist approach, this essay will show that although many of the worries surrounding Ritalin consumption in children are ill-founded the use of Ritalin in grade school children should be banned since no data is available concerning the long-term side effects of the drug. In order to achieve this, an explanation of what ADHD is exactly, as well as discussion of what is believed to cause the disorder will be given. This background information will eliminate many possible misconceptions and will enable a better understanding of what should be the central ethical debate surrounding the use of Ritalin in children.

Writing a Paragraph

A well written paragraph should start with **a transition word or sentence**; it should have a **clear topic sentence** and because this is a thesis essay, the topic sentence of your paragraph should be one of your premises and most importantly, there should **only be one idea per paragraph**.

As you are writing, you should always ensure that you have adequate flow between your sentences. Using transition words can help you achieve this.

Here is a list of transition words that you can use:

To begin	Also	Consequently
Initially	In addition	Besides
Originally	Moreover	As well
First	Second	To continue
First of all	Additionally	Furthermore

You should also **ensure that you are not producing critical thinking errors** (see chapter 6 and 7 for more information on this) particularly the circularity fallacy. Consider the following example, which is a paragraph that tries to provide a premise as to why animal testing is wrong:

Example 48

To begin with, animal testing is not always accurate. According to global active news line, "reactions can vary greatly from species to species so it is quite difficult to come to any conclusions about what a substance will do to humans by testing it on a rabbit." (Global Active News line, 2007, p. 4) From this, it is clear that the results of the tests are pretty much unreliable and pointless. Because the results are not always accurate, animal testing should not be done.

In the above example, no information is given to support the premise. In fact, the premise is simply repeated several times but worded differently. Also, it should be noted that using a quote from a figure of authority on the issue that asserts your premise or thesis will not do as this too creates the circularity fallacy (see p. 61 for more information on this fallacy). You need to ensure that you are presenting facts and information that support and explain WHY your premise is true.

Consider the following example:

Example 49

To begin with, animal testing is not always accurate. According to Kelly Overton, an executive director of People Protecting Animals and Their Habitats, "animal testing proved penicillin deadly, strychnine safe and aspirin dangerous" (Overton, 2006, p1). In fact, an alarming 90% of medications approved for human use after animal testing later proved ineffective or harmful to humans in clinical trials (Overton, 2006, p.1). Because humans and animals have different physiologies, reactions can vary greatly from species to species so it is quite difficult to come to any conclusions about what a substance will do to humans by testing it on an animal (Global Active News line, 2007, p. 4).

In this example, the quote serves to provide a few examples that SHOW that animal testing is not always accurate. There is also information given as to the rate of inaccuracy and an explanation for this inaccuracy. This paragraph is not circular at all as facts are given to support the topic sentence.

Once your paragraph is done, you can add a transition sentence that will lead into your next premise. However, if you choose to do this, you should ensure that you are not breaking the flow of your essay and that you are actually creating a smooth transition.

Writing a Conclusion

Your conclusion should also start with a transition word (see p.13 for a list of transition words that could be used). It should also recap the main points of your essay. At a very minimum, you need to ensure that you have restated your main premises as well as your thesis statement. Finally, you should end your essay with a question or comment that suggests how your topic and thesis could be furthered. In essence, you need a closing statement.

Visualizing an essay

If you are more of a visual or mathematical person, then this is what your essay should look like:

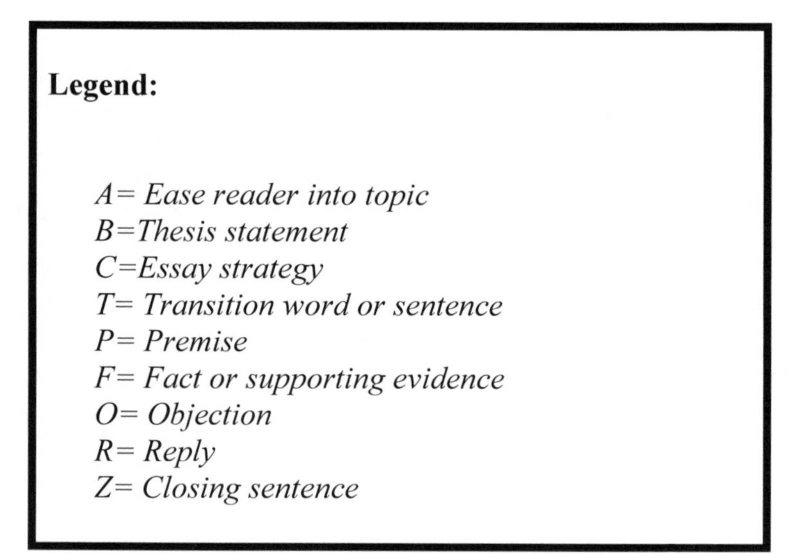

Legend:

A= Ease reader into topic
B=Thesis statement
C=Essay strategy
T= Transition word or sentence
P= Premise
F= Fact or supporting evidence
O= Objection
R= Reply
Z= Closing sentence

Example 50

Introduction:

A
B
C

Body

T	*P1*
F1	
F2	
F3	

T	*P2*
F1	
F2	
F3	

T	*P3*
F1	
F2	
F3	

Objection and Reply

T	*O*
R	

Conclusion

T	*P1*
P2	
P3	
B	
Z	

Or, you can also have the following structure:

Example 51

Introduction:

A
B
C

Body

T	*F1*
F2	
F3	
P1	

T	*F1*
F2	
F3	
P2	

T	*F1*
F2	
F3	
P3	

Objection and reply

T	*O*
R	

Conclusion

T	*P1*
P2	
P3	
B	
Z	

Once you have written a draft of your essay, you should let it sit for a few hours (ideally a day). You should ask a friend to proofread your work and then you should write your final version. Here is a checklist that might be useful when proofreading your essay.

Essay checklist:

	Y	*N*
1. Do I present an argument that defends my position on the topic chosen?		
2. Do I have at least three premises?		
3. Does my first premise respect the following critical thinking rules?		
a. Does not contain any fallacies		
b. Does not contain any deceptive statistics		
c. Does not contain any unreliable figure of authority		
d. Does not contain claims that would need justification		
e. Does not contain claims that are vague or ambiguous		
f. Does not contain claims where counter examples could be found		
g. Does not contain any false information		
h. Helps support the conclusion (is relevant)		
i. Does not violate any other rule of reasoning		
j. Do I provide enough evidence to accept the premise		
4. Does my second premise respect the following critical thinking rules?		
a. Does not contain any fallacies		
b. Does not contain any deceptive statistics		
c. Does not contain any unreliable figure of authority		

d. Does not contain claims that would need justification		
e. Does not contain claims that are vague or ambiguous		
f. Does not contain claims where counter examples could be found		
g. Does not contain any false information		
h. Helps support the conclusion (is relevant)		
i. Does not violate any other rule of reasoning		
j. Do I provide enough evidence to accept the premise		
5. Does my third premise respect the following critical thinking rules?		
a. Does not contain any fallacies		
b. Does not contain any deceptive statistics		
c. Does not contain any unreliable figure of authority		
d. Does not contain claims that would need justification		
e. Does not contain claims that are vague or ambiguous		
f. Does not contain claims where counter examples could be found		
g. Does not contain any false information		
h. Helps support the conclusion (is relevant)		
i. Does not violate any other rule of reasoning		
j. Do I provide enough evidence to accept the premise		
6. Do I have an introduction that eases the reader into the topic before stating the thesis?		
7. Does my introduction represent about 10% of my essay?		
8. Do I have a nice flow in my introduction—does it reflect college level writing skills?		
9. Do I have a clear thesis statement in my introduction?		
10. Do I have paragraphs?		
11. Do I only develop one idea per paragraph?		

	Y	***N***
12. Do I have a topic sentence for each paragraph?		
13. Do I have a transition word or sentence for each paragraph?		
14. Is there a nice flow in the essay—does it reflect college level writing skills?		
15. Are my ideas presented in a logical order?		
16. Do I have a conclusion?		
17. Does my conclusion recap the main points of my essay?		
18. Do I restate my thesis in my conclusion?		
19. Do I have an ending comment in my conclusion?		
20. Is there a nice flow in my conclusion—does it reflect college level writing skills?		
21. Did I use an appropriate amount of **references** *within the body of this essay?*		
22. Did I reference all information that is not common knowledge, all paraphrases and quotes?		
23. Did I use the referencing style that my teacher asked me to use (APA, MLA, Chicago)?		
24. Did I ensure that all my sources are credible and reliable?		
25. Did I proofread my essay to ensure that there are no language mistakes left?		
26. Did I ask someone to proofread my essay?		
27. Did I ensure that I followed all of my teacher's instructions?		
28. Is my work stapled?		

ANSWERS TO SELECTED EXERCISES

Exercises Chapter 2---- Answers

1. Questions
3. Argument
    a. Because we do not know the original context of the writings
    b. Seeing as we only have passages and not complete works,
    c. Therefore, it is very difficult to be certain of the actual intentions of Pre-Socratic philosophers.
5. Explanation
7. Emotions (or opinion)
9. Description
11. Argument
    a. In 2005 it was estimated that there were about 1 282 780 149 Muslims, 856 690 863 Hindus and 381 610 979 Buddhists.
    b. Christianity has an estimated total of 2 116 909 552 adherents,
    c. Therefore, Christianity is the most popular religion in the world.
13. Fact
15. Description (or facts)
17. Question
19. Explanation
21. Explanation
23. Fact
25. Argument
    a. There are more sexually explicit scenes on TV today than there were 40 years ago.
    b. Today's children are sexually active at a much younger age
    c. Therefore, television is responsible for our youth's promiscuity.

Exercises Chapter 3---- Answers

1.
   a. The argument is not valid (because the premises do not say that all men are like Socrates…)
   b. The premises are True
   c. The argument is not sound (because the argument is not valid)

3.
   a. The argument is valid (premises support the conclusion)
   b. Premise 2 is not true (only the men that were wise were considered philosophers in ancient Greece--- only a select few fell within this category)
   c. The argument is not sound (because there is at least one false premise)

5.
   a. The argument is valid (the premises support the conclusion)
   b. The premises are True
   c. The argument is sound (because the argument is valid and the premises are true)

7.
   a. The argument is valid (the premises support the conclusion)
   b. Premise 2 is not true (Picasso was born in Spain and not China)
   c. The argument is not sound (because there is at least one false premise)

9.
   a. The argument is not valid (because the premises do not say that all Latin Americans know how to dance Salsa)
   b. The premises are True
   c. The argument is not sound (because the argument is not valid)

11.
   a. The argument is valid (the premises support the conclusion)
   b. The premises are True
   c. The argument is sound (because the argument is valid and the premises are true

13.

a. The argument is not valid (The premises do not support the conclusion. The fact that Patrick is in a noisy and chaotic place does not mean that he is praying. The premise does not say that when one is in such a place that they automatically pray.)
b. Premise 1 is not true and who knows who and where Patrick is
c. The argument is not sound (because the argument is not valid and there is at least one false premise)

15.

a. The argument is not valid (The premises do not support the conclusion. It does not say that all terrorists are Muslims)
b. Premise 1 is not true and we do not know who and what Abdul is
c. The argument is not sound (because the argument is not valid and there is at least one false premise)

17.

a. The argument is not valid (knowing how many sides a triangle or square has does tell us anything about how many sides a pentagon has)
b. The premises are True
c. The argument is not sound (because the argument is not valid)

19.

a. The argument is not valid (The premises do not support the conclusion. The fact that Prostitution is studied does not mean it is a science)
b. Premise 3 is not true
c. The argument is not sound (because the argument is not valid and there is at least one false premise)

21.

a. The argument is valid (the premises support the conclusion)
b. The premises are True
c. The argument is sound (because the argument is valid and the premises are true)

23.

a. The argument is not valid (The premises do not support the conclusion. It does not say that ALL highly intelligent people know how to use the Internet.)
b. Premise 1 is not true
c. The argument is not sound (because the argument is not valid and there is at least one false premise)

25.

a. The argument is valid (the premises support the conclusion)
b. The premises are True
c. The argument is sound (because the argument is valid and the premises are true)

Exercises Chapter 4---- Answers

1. Deductive (is based on how definition of man)
3. Deductive (is based on definition of where Miletus is)
5. Deductive (is based on how one relates to the other, not on frequency of occurrence)
7. Inductive (is based on probability considering that all others are worth a lot of money)
9. Deductive (is based on definition of sculpture)
11. Inductive (is based on probability that if the few I spoke to are Muslims then all others are too)
13. Inductive (is based on frequency—the idea that he has always gone)
15. Deductive (is based on how religious is defined)
17. Inductive (Newton figured it out because he saw it happen all the time… However, this does not mean that it will always be the case. If the earth stops turning, then there will no longer be gravity. This is like the "sun coming up" example.
19. Deductive (is based on how a km is defined in relation to meters….)
21. Inductive (The weather channel bases its information on predictions-- it is a % of chance of rain or sun… a probability)
23. Inductive (you hope that because a station usually plays that kind of music that you will fall upon your song. It is a probability --- not a certainty)

25. Deductive (There are 12 months in a year and you pay a certain amount per month. So x times 12 months will give you your amount. That is how a yearly cost is defined.)

Exercises Chapter 5---- Answers

1. Not acceptable: Needs figure of authority (information is not common knowledge and hence needs a reference)
3. Not acceptable: Vague or Ambiguous (this is an opinion, what is not useful to one could be very useful to another).
5. Not acceptable: Can find a counter-example—Aristotle, Plato, Socrates, Thales are a few examples that can be given to show the statement wrong)
7. Acceptable: Considering that the information given is about who was on Oprah, in this situation, the Oprah website is reliable.
9. Not acceptable: Contradiction
11. Not acceptable: Needs a reference
13. Acceptable: Common knowledge
15. Not acceptable: Blogs are not reliable sources
17. Not acceptable: A priori false (a triangle is defined as having three sides)
19. Acceptable: Supported by relevant figure of authority from reliable website (academic database and peer-reviewed journal)
21. Acceptable: Common knowledge
23. Not acceptable: Can find counter example—*Fashion Magazine* is another one that is sold in North America
25. Not acceptable: The Internet source is not reliable

Exercises Chapter 6---- Answers

1. *Ad hominem* (when he lived has no bearing on the truth value of his claims)
3. False dilemma (there are many other philosophers that you could enjoy)
5. Hasty generalization
7. Slippery slope

9. Equivocation (with the words dark, light and lighter atmosphere)
11. Hasty generalization
13. Popularity
15. Equivocation (with the word cause)
17. Slippery Slope
19. Appeal to pity
21. False dilemma
23. Generalization
25. *Ad hominem*

Exercises Chapter 7---- Answers

1. Biased sample
3. Size of sample
5. Unreliable statistics (Not clear that people would admit this)
7. Confusing average (if the average is 700, then there are some that are much more expensive than that---just like there are some that are much cheaper too.)
9. Deceiving by omitting information (Bigger than what?)
11. Proving one thing concluding another (They might all be referring to the same criminal. A better study would give % of religious people who are in prison vs. non-religious)
13 .Size of sample
15. Year of sample (the number of members changed since 1978)
17. Deceiving by omitting information (faster than what?)
19. Size of sample
21. Unreliable statistics
23. Year of sample
25. Size of sample

Exercises Chapter 8---- Answers

Pablo Picasso's value

1. Argument:
   a. Picasso was famous
   b. Picasso created cubism
   c. Picasso sold the most expensive art piece ever
   d. Therefore, Picasso's art has great value
2. Deductive logic (is based on how things are defined)
3. Argument analysis:
   a. The argument is valid—There is a logical connection. If the premises are true, then the conclusion cannot be false. If he did sell the most expensive piece of art ever, then this means that his art has great value.
   b. Are the premises acceptable?
      i. Premise 1:
         1. Circularity fallacy: famous because art has great value and art has great value because he is famous.
         2. Popularity fallacy: Using Facebook
         3. Hasty generalization fallacy: 24 people on Facebook discussing something does not make it true.
      ii. Premise 2:
         1. Red Herring fallacy: explaining what cubism is does not explain why it made him famous.
         2. Contradiction: If creating cubism made him famous, then Braque should be just as famous.
      iii. Premise 3:
         1. Year of sample: 2004 is a long time ago. Many art pieces have been sold since then and with a bit of research, you will find that his record was broken. (A note, although the statement is false, the fact that it sold for so much money certainly says something about the value of his art)
         2. Red Herring fallacy: Being 24 does not help justify the premise (perhaps if it was done when he was 10…)

Since the premises are not properly justified, the argument is quite weak and cannot be sound.

4. Does not apply.

The truth about cell phones

1. Argument:
   a. Using a cell phone increases your chance of getting a brain tumour
   b. Using a cell phone leads to premature loss of hearing in adults
   c. Cell phones are bad for the environment
   d. Therefore, cell phones should not be manufactured or sold to teenagers
2. Inductive logic (is based on observations in the world and frequency of occurrence (of brain tumours and hearing loss…)
3. Does not apply
4. Argument analysis:
   a. The logical connection is interesting but it is strange that it discusses effects in adults, yet concludes that they should not be sold to teenagers (as opposed to "not sold to anyone at all"
   b. Are the premises Acceptable?
      i. Premise 1:
         1. Deceiving by omitting information: 12% of what? How many people were getting brain tumours before cell phones? Did we go from 10 to 11 per year?
         2. Circularity fallacy: The paragraph simply repeats in several different ways that it increases chances of brain tumour. It does not give justification
      ii. Premise 2:
         1. Popularity fallacy: Tom Hanks
         2. Hasty Generalization: One person is not enough
         3. Proving one thing, concluding another: The fact that hearing loss rates have gone up does not necessarily mean that it is because of cell phones. There are several other possible explanations (use of ear phones, loud music in discotheques…).
      iii. Premise 3:
         1. Slippery slope: … will lead to human death toll…
         2. Hasty Generalization: Odif is only one of many (and this would need a reference)

Since all premises are not properly justified, none are acceptable. Considering that there is a problem with the logical connection and all premises, this is a very weak argument.

Bibliography

Bergmann, M., Moor, J., Nelson, J. (1998). *The logic Book, third edition.* Montreal: McGraw-Hill.

Blackburn, P. (1989). *Logique de l'argumentation.* Montreal: ERPI

Browne, M.N. & Keeley, S. (2004). *Asking the right questions; a guide to critical thinking, seventh edition.* New Jersey: Pearson Prentice Hall.

Buchholz E., Bühler G., Hille K., Kaeppele S. and Stotland I.. (2007). *ART a world history*, New York; Abrams

CBC Marketplace (1998, November 3). *Getting a grip: Are your all-season tires really equipped?* Retrieved May 3, 2005 from http://www.cbc.ca/consumers/ market/files/cars/tires/

CBC Marketplace (1998 , November 3). *Putting tires to the test.* Retrieved May 3, 2005 from http://www.cbc.ca /consumers/market/files/cars/tires/tiretests.html

CBC News Online (2004, December 8). *Winter Tires: Making a comeback.* Retrieved May 3, 2005 from http://www.cbc.ca /news/background/consumertips/ wintertires.html

Digital Dream Door (2009). *The Best Jokes: Socrates the Great Philosopher.* Retrieved February 20, 2010 from http://digitaldreamdoor.nusie.com/pages/quotes/ best_jokes2.html

Auguste-Rodin. (No Date) *Encyclopedia Britannica online.* Retrieved February 20, 2010, from http:// www.britannica.com

Etkin, David (No date) The Social and Economic Impact of Hydrometeorological Hazards and Disasters: a Preliminary Inventory. Coping with Natural Hazards in Canada: Scientific, Government and Insurance Industry Perspectives; part 2: natural hazards in Canada Retreived May 3, 2005 from http://www.utoronto.ca/env/nh/pt2ch4-4.htm

Epstein, R. (1999). *Critical thinking.* Toronto: Wadsworth Publishing Company.

Epstein, R. (1999). Workbook for *critical thinking.* Toronto: Wadsworth Publishing Company

Fearnside, W. (1997). *About thinking, second edition.* New Jersey: Prentice Hall.

Govier, T. (2001). *A practical study of argument, fifth edition.* Canada: Wadsworth Thomson Learning.

Gross, Joel (2010) Religion Facts. *Best Online Marketing Site- Joel Gross.* Retrieved February 20, 2010, from http://www.blog.joelx.com/religion-facts/627

Grunau, B. and Olson, J. (2010) An interesting presentation of pediatric tetanus. *The Journal of the Canadian Association of Emergency Physicians* 12(1) p. 70. Retrieved form Academic Search Premier database. (Accession No. 47813426)

Jensen, Cheryl (2004, December 5). *Getting a grip on snow with the right tires.* Retrieved May 3, 2005 from http://www.stangbangers.com/Snow_Tires.htm

Mega Essays (2010). Retrieved February 20, 2010, from http://www.megaessays.com

Oprah (2008) *Oprah goes One-on-One with Tom Cruise in a Two-Part Oprah Show Special.* Retrieved February 20, 2010 from http://www.oprah.com/pressroom/Oprah-Goes-One-on-One-with -Tom-Cruise-in-Two-Part-Special

Radio Canada (2004, January 30). *Aujourd'hui.* Retrieved May 3, 2005 from http://radio-canada.ca/actualite/placepublique /messages.asp?clip=862

Ruggiero, V. (2002). *Becoming a critical thinker, fourth edition.* Boston: Houghton Mifflin Company.

SAAQ (2004, 1e trimestre) Avez-vous les bons pneus pour déjouer l'hiver? *Info SAAQ Bulletin no 4.* Retrieved May 3, 2005 fromhttp://www.saaq.gouv.qc.ca/publications/prevention/info saaq /infosaaq_04f.pdf

Vaidehi (2010) Technology Facts abut the world of Technology. Scientific Facts from the Science World!---*LASER*. Retrieved on February 20, 2010 from http://tech-fact.blogspot.com

Walton, D. & Woods, J. (1982). *Argument: the logic of the fallacies*. Montreal: McGraw-Hill Ryerson Limited.